FINDING

ST. LO

A Memoir of War and Family

By

GORDON EDWARD CROSS

ROBERT LEWIS FOWLER

TED NEILL (Editor)

Dedicated to the men of the 35th Infantry Division
and the families who loved and mourned them.

And in acknowledgment of the *Chaticks si Chaticks*, the
"Men of Men," aka the Pawnee—the original settlers of the
plains and lands of the Loup and Platte Rivers. It was their
spirit that inspired the motto of the 134th Infantry Regiment:
La We La His – The Strong, the Brave

THE OMAHA WORLD HERALD

THE 35TH TROOPS STOPPED HITLER'S BEST TROOPS

September 13, 1944

Somewhere in France—The brilliant and effective role that the 35th Infantry Division has played in the liberation of France is officially revealed. Punching and smashing down the center of the Cherbourg peninsula, the division drove home the blows which, in a large measure, broke the back of the German resistance in Normandy. It has spearheaded through battle areas where the bitterness and ferocity of combat has been unequaled by American troops in this theater, except at the beach-heads.

The division, which arrived in England last May 26, was first committed in the *La Meuffe* area, on July 9. From there its troops, absorbing everything that the well-entrenched and determined enemy could offer, smashed past Emile and across bloody Hill No. 122 in combat featured by hand-to-hand fighting.

The division's frontal attack was the decisive factor in the capture of St. Lo—here again the enemy was thrown out of an entrenched position he had every intention of holding. From St. Lo, division forces pushed across heavily defended Hill No. 101. Under heavy artillery, mortar and tank fire, the 35th captured *Torigni Sur Vire,* and battled onward until it had overrun the key defense positions at the base of the Cherbourg peninsula.

Moving southward, the division, in the words of its chief of staff, was literally "thumbed off the road," to stop the German thrust toward *Avranches.* In five days of intensive fighting in the *Mortain* area it slammed shut the door and smothered the Germans' last important effort in France. Hitler's best SS troops were stopped cold in their effort to drive to the sea and divide American armies.

After the battle of *Mortain,* the division staged a spectacular "road map dash" through the heart of France. Some units covered well over a hundred miles in a day. This dash terminated with the capture of *Cloyes, Chateaudun,* and *Orleans,* all taken in a day. Within a few days the division captured more than 3,500 prisoners.

The 35th attacked on thirty-five of its forty-five days in combat. The division was mobilized for the present emergency on December 23, 1940. It was made up of units of the Kansas, Nebraska, and Missouri National Guard units. A year later it was assigned to defend the Southern California Coast. On April 1, 1943, it moved to Camp Rucker, Ala. On November 15th, it moved to Tennessee for maneuvers. In January 1944, it moved to Camp Butner, NC, for final training. It arrived in France July 6-7.

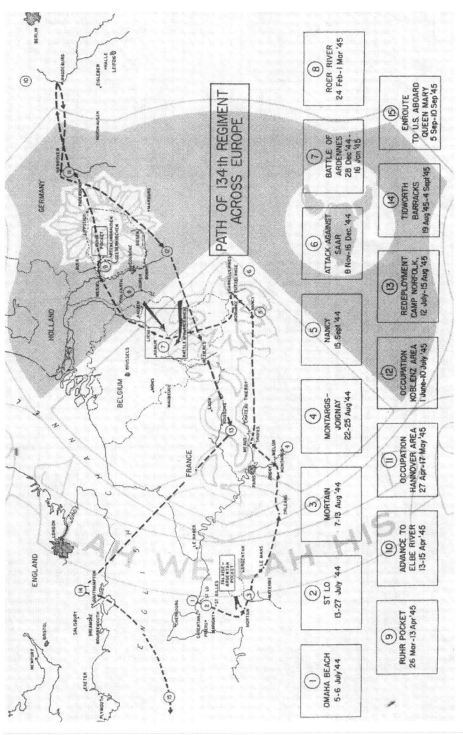

PATH OF 134th REGIMENT ACROSS EUROPE

① OMAHA BEACH 5-6 July '44

② ST LO 13-27 July '44

③ MORTAIN 7-13 Aug '44

④ MONTARGIS - JOIGNAY 22-25 Aug '44

⑤ NANCY 15 Sept '44

⑥ ATTACK AGAINST SAAR 8 Nov-16 Dec '44

⑦ BATTLE OF ARDENNES 28 Dec '44 - 16 Jan '45

⑧ ROER RIVER 24 Feb - 1 Mar '45

⑨ RUHR POCKET 26 Mar - 13 Apr '45

⑩ ADVANCE TO ELBE RIVER 13-15 Apr '45

⑪ OCCUPATION HANNOVER AREA 27 Apr-17 May '45

⑫ OCCUPATION KOBLENZ AREA 1 June-10 July '45

⑬ REDEPLOYMENT CAMP NORFOLK, 12 July-15 Aug '45

⑭ TIDWORTH BARRACKS 19 Aug '45-4 Sept '45

⑮ ENROUTE TO U.S. ABOARD QUEEN MARY 5 Sep-10 Sep '45

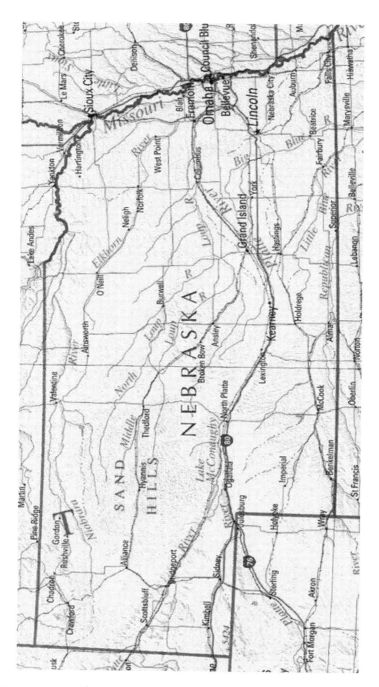

Maps Curtesy of 134th Infantry Regiment Website & Public Domain Maps

PART I

Robert Lewis Fowler: Recollections of a GI

REFLECTIONS I.
Grampa Fowler
Ted Neill

I only ever had one Grampa. That was Bob Fowler. "Grampa" was what I and all his other grandchildren called him. Like everyone else, I, of course, had two grand*fathers*—but I had only one "Grampa."

Robert Lewis Fowler was my mother's father. My dad's father, Charles Waggaman Neill, was appropriately named "Dad's Daddy" since (I'm told) I met Grampa Fowler first and wholeheartedly accepted him as "Grampa" and insisted ever after (as only children with zero tolerance for ambiguity can) that there could be only one Grampa.

"Grampa Neill" was not to be.

But Grampa Fowler, Major Robert Lewis Fowler, "Bob," was a challenge for me and for all of his family. He was never just one thing. Who is? But Grampa, as an individual man of his era, a symbol of his generation, and even as an archetype of the warrior, defied easy categorization, to say the least, characterization.

Grampa Fowler was, without a doubt, a war hero. He was a man who faced the crucible of battle, bearing witness to the horrors of modern warfare. The carnage of World War II was not abstract to him. For a few weeks in the summer of 1944, he was anointed from head to toe with the mud, dirt, and shit of battle, not to mention blood—his blood and his comrades' blood—as munitions blew men, *his friends*, into pieces alongside him. This violence would wound his body, break his heart, and shatter his psyche.

Robert Lewis Fowler was a father. A grandfather. A son. A brother. A husband. He was a handsome, steely-faced, taciturn midwestern man. A slow talker. So much so, that you could interject complete sentences in the lacunas between his words—if you dared to interrupt him. But no one ever did, not even my fast-talking, polyglot father, raised in New Jersey, a man who had attended elite boarding schools on the East Coast and centuries-old universities in Europe. Nervous, fast talking was in his bloodstream, even when he had nothing useful to say. But even he learned to slow down and settle into Grampa's flow.

Grampa's slow talk never came off as indicative of a slow mind. You never doubted for an instant that there was a keen intellect behind Grandpa's eyes. They were piercing, honed like the sharpshooter and map reader that he was. His gaze was steady, accustomed to long drives along highways with bleached, baked, and battered asphalt. These were ribbons of road cracked by the weight of winter snows, scoured by spring storms, and hammered by summer sun. These long routes trace lines across a prairie that imposes silence between travelers. Small towns are separated by space *and* time, hours of travel along unbroken vistas of grass rolling on hills like ocean swells and spangled with wild flowers. The scope of it all is dwarfed only by the big sky that even sunsets and mountain ranges of cumulonimbus can't fill.

You just understood in Grampa's presence that he had his own cadence. He moved at his own pace, as if tied to the earth he had grown up hoeing, sowing, reaping and baling upon. This pace was not agitated. It was never nervous. And in Grampa's presence, as if by force of his own gravity, you simply fell into his rhythm. You didn't question; you just accepted. It was a restorative surrender, a bit like how I imagined Huck Finn and Jim, pushed along in their raft in the Mississippi; or just reading the actual novel, riding along on Mark Twain's words, the pace of the plot all his, not yours. You'll get to your destination, sure as the river flows and the page turns. You never doubt that. The laws of nature guarantee it. Just keep floating. Just keep flipping. But ultimately, we are powerless as to when we will arrive—at our destination, at the conclusion and whatever resolution it brings (if any). So, you wait, you float, you move word by word. You let the flow move things around you. You watch. You observe. Most of all, you listen. It's a way of being that, today, I fear we have mainly lost.

As a result, you felt calm in Grampa's presence. Safe. He was reassuring. I could see how men would want to follow him. Impervious. Unflappable. This natural calm translated into an aura of authority, a calm in battle and a sangfroid even before 4-star generals who would come to review him and his company. Grampa's commanding officers always positioned him in a place where the generals coming for review would encounter him first, hoping they might speak with him and he represent the company of men. They knew Grampa was respectful of authority but never flustered by it.

Grampa's presence loomed large for those of us in his family, just as his generation occupies a prominent place in twentieth century history. His story, his heroism, his endurance, signified by the campaign bars, the bronze star, and the purple heart that lined his medal case. His generation's grit honored with titles such as "Greatest."

But there was more to Robert Lewis Fowler. In addition to these identities, there were other, darker ones. He was a careless, reckless, belligerent drunk. At times, so was his wife Evelyn.

Grampa was a neglectful father, an unfaithful husband, a disappointment to his children, and a wreck of a man. These were shadow identities for Grampa, shadows his grandchildren only saw themselves towards the end of his life. We mostly knew him during the decades he was sober. It was *mostly* in imagination that we knew this side of him even existed. Growing up, we heard that past times had been worse and that there were rifts yet to be healed. But this knowledge came secondhand, through the stories shared by my aunts.

The evidence of shadows also lay in my mother's own journey. My mother, Kathleen, was the oldest of eight children. Once grown, she moved from her hometown of Omaha, Nebraska, to Washington, DC, to flee from her family and the chaos of her parents' relationship. But that, having taken place before I was born, always seemed like ancient history to me.

These stories of Grampa and Evelyn's dark times were not volunteered freely. My cousins and I only caught bits and pieces, either through unexpected admissions or casual asides. These were breadcrumbs for us to follow at our own risk.

My mother once spoke of coming home from college to find the youngest two children, Joe and Sally, playing with broken beer bottles in place of toys. My aunt Mary Anne described Grampa picking her up at a friend's house once blind drunk. He drove her home, speeding and swerving through the streets of downtown Omaha at a time when seatbelts were not commonplace. By some miracle they made it home, bouncing over the curb, the car coming to a stop on the lawn before Grampa staggered out to sleep it off in the grass.

There were times Mom laughed and said she came from "white-trash." Other times, she cried.

Over time, I learned that my own mother's attachment to my childhood home was even in reaction to her itinerant childhood. She and my father purchased their home in 1980 and have lived there since, never moving or relocating. I spent the entirety of my formative years in that home. But more importantly, that house has been a home to my mother longer than any other because, growing up, her parents were constantly being evicted from one house, then another—for drunken behavior, property damage, delinquent payments, too many children, or all four.

The stories Mom told of these years were sparse, but the pain was all too apparent. I glimpsed it when she spoke of telling her father "no" shortly before Christmas one year when he once called asking for money. He said they needed it to keep the heat and lights on.

Mom had established her own career as a nurse by that point in her life. She was independent and free. But she was torn apart by the idea of her youngest two siblings, Joe and Sally, living in such privation. But she knew she could not trust her father to follow through and spend any money she sent to him on her siblings. Sending anything, she knew, just enabled his drinking. Mom was also worried that Evelyn's depression was manifesting as continued drinking and even reckless gambling.

It was only as an adult that I understood that my mother's almost obsessive passion for Christmas grew out of this as well. Her over-the-top decorations and gift-giving were her own efforts of overcompensation for the Christmases she'd never had. She was determined that, as her son, I would never have Christmas memories even remotely like hers. Memories of a home without presents, or even a tree, *or even adults,* as they were still out drinking or passed out come Christmas morning.

I sometimes pictured my mother's heart as a duplex home, with two adjacent living spaces that were entirely separate from one another—separate entrances, separate exits—where the fondness and attachment in one unit never interacted or even acknowledged the neighbors in the next. The love and commitment to family lived in protective ignorance of the hurts, the disappointments, the still simmering resentment and anger lodged just next door.

But there was no such dividing wall for me. As a result, all these conflicting images of her family formed a confusing mixture for me. Mom, in self-imposed exile on the East Coast, would describe Omaha, Nebraska, and the Midwest in general in glowing terms. It was a place of golden fields, unconstrained sunsets, and "good" people. Mom always seemed genuinely perplexed when I'd express ambivalence about visiting my relatives there, as if she had not been the one to tell me about her parents' alcoholism, her siblings' alcoholism, and the continuing legacy of addiction and mental health disorders tearing up the bodies and psyches of some of my cousins.

I was afraid that if I went there, I might end up the same. After all, wasn't that why she left?

Youth does not tolerate paradox, much less complexity, very well. So, over time, I tamped these misgivings down. It wasn't hard. My interactions with Omaha family were overwhelmingly positive. As an only child, my cousins were the siblings I never had. And throughout my formative years, Grampa and Grandma Evelyn had decades of unbroken sobriety. As I was growing up, they were loving, welcome visitors to our home in Northern Virginia. They would never fly, because Grampa still loved cars and still loved driving. So they drove from Nebraska to Virginia, stopping and visiting old war buddies along the way.

Grandma Evelyn was funny, irreverent, and long suffering for all Bob had put her through, but no less witty or smart for it. I enjoyed how she poked at my own father—the primary authority figure in my life—reducing him to the role of placating and stammering son-in-law. Despite her badgering of him, I knew my dad also had a deep respect for Grandma Evelyn. Her affection was expressed in her quips and his in taking the jabs, letting her needle him for his posh background, his expansive education, and his command of multiple languages, all of which she secretly admired.

On my parents' wedding day, Evelyn chided my father—who always had a dark five o'clock shadow—saying, "You could have at least shaved for your wedding day," followed by a reminder that, "You'll never be my favorite son-in-law."

Yet for all Evelyn's picking on him, it was my father she asked to give her eulogy as one of her final requests before passed away in 1991.

The shadow identities of Grampa Bob and Grandma Evelyn continued to fade as I grew older. After Evelyn died, Grampa remarried a redheaded woman who was charming but wise enough to insist that we call her by her lifelong nickname of Coco . . . and *not* Grandma. There was no replacing Grandma Evelyn and never would be.

Coco, with her own feistiness, seemed to smooth out Grampa's last rough edges, getting him to drop his own lifelong habit of cigar smoking, as well as his long-enduring habit of trading in his "old" car for a new one every twelve to eighteen months. These departures from long-established patterns shocked many of us who had known him and thought him incapable of further change.

But in those last years, when I was in college, the shadows returned.

As any drunk familiar with the literature and meetings of Alcoholics Anonymous will tell you, alcoholism is a progressive and fatal disease. You are *never* cured. Even while you are sober, you are still just an "alcoholic between drinks." Even as you string one day after another . . . into weeks . . . into months . . . even into years, the milestones commemorated with coins and hugs at meetings celebrating AA sobriety birthdays . . . your addiction is still within you. It's *never* dormant. You are *never* cured. Your addiction is bench pressing and cross-training, as drunks in recovery say. It's even doing pushups in the parking lot, ready to pounce on you after every meeting you attend. It is diligently preparing and ever vigilant for the moment of weakness, when you are susceptible to a slip, then a relapse, or as members of AA call it, "Going back out there."

Many don't make it back. Progressive disease means *progressive*. Addiction comes back just as bad, often worse, than it ever was before. It's all the harder to overcome again, especially for those alcoholics who have lived a long life of unbroken sobriety: recoverees who, in older age, their minds and bodies not as strong as they once were, go out and get drunk again. To their shock, they find out they still had one more drunk left in them—but not one more recovery. That is when the disease seizes you again, throttling your life, your will, your well-being, and all your relationships with a force you thought had all but disappeared.

And that is why they say, if you are going to be a member of AA, you should also have a black suit always pressed and ready. You'll need it for the funerals. Not everyone makes it. It's a cold, hard fact.

As a result, members of Alcoholics Anonymous will always tell you that the most important person at any meeting is the newcomer. Not only because they need love and support in the early stages of their recovery, but because old timers need to be reminded of the chaos, suffering, and heartbreak that is just one sip away. . . .

And so it was with Grampa. In his last years, Bob Fowler had a number of "slips." After an operation to remove a cancerous kidney, the incisions stubbornly refused to heal. His abdomen became enlarged, and many of us worried that he was drinking in secret. The site of the procedure turned into jagged wounds that wept infected puss and poorly circulated blood. His life was literally draining away.

When he suffered a stroke in April 2006, he did not have the reserves to recover, and he died shortly after.

We grandchildren had only known Grampa as a charming, benevolent, chuckling old man. Bob Fowler, war hero, with his full shock of thick white hair even into old age. Now we had the uncomfortable task of trying to reconcile these two Robert Fowlers: the heroic patriarch and the irascible, swaying drunk. His five surviving daughters made the adjustment seamlessly. Their old defense mechanisms and coping strategies proved to be still intact. Those protective barriers returned in full force, so much so that Bob's daughters didn't even seem to register the cognitive dissonance generated among their children or the distress it entailed. For me and my cousins, never having had a "wall" between two Omahas, two versions of Robert Fowler, we felt like we'd lost Grampa even before he physically died. Some twisted, distorted impostor with a ruptured abdomen, a swollen liver, and a face flushed with rosacea took his place. A grump who was by turns surly or explosive.

We just wanted the Grampa we knew back.

I didn't know how to fix any of it, or how to make sense of it. None of us did. I thought I would carry this sense of loss, this unresolved contradiction, for the rest of my life. I understood, on reflection, that both impressions of Bob Fowler were part of a whole, a whole I had never really seen for myself until the end. But my experiences of Robert Lewis Fowler in life were insufficient to understand him in death.

But then there was the memoir.

REFLECTIONS II.
The Memoir
Ted Neill

Grampa had talked about the war to me throughout my life. I knew him as a man defined by his war service. I drew pictures of battles for him with crayons when I was as young as five—the historical accuracy was dubious at best, as I recall substituting X-Wings for P-38 Lightnings. Despite the mishmash of Star Wars and World Wars, I remember Grampa receiving the artwork with graciousness.

My earliest memories of him are sitting next to him as we paged through books on the war while he pointed out his friends and himself in black and white photos. As a nascent writer, I gravitated to him and his narrative. Even then, I recognized his story as something epic.

Through high school and college, I recounted his war stories to any friends who would listen, especially as films and miniseries such as *Saving Private Ryan*, *The Thin Red Line,* and *Band of Brothers* brought depictions of the war into the mainstream. The black and white version of WWII on the History Channel was updated with sound effects and computer-generated imagery.

I faithfully wore a watch Grampa gifted to me with the seal of his regiment, the 134th, on its face. It bore the motto of the regiment: *La Wi La His*—Pawnee for "The Strong and the Brave." While in college I wore a leather jacket he'd handed down to me that was an exact replica of the military-issue jacket he wore throughout his years of service. He had ordered it through a vintage catalogue, only to find that I matched his wartime measurements a bit better than he did, fifty-five years later.

He ordered the next size up for the replacement.

It was probably a bit of Grampa's influence that helped me to win Veterans of Foreign War (VFW) essay contests on patriotism while in high school. This earned me my own medals, which Grampa would talk about to anyone who would listen.

Then came June 1994. It was the fiftieth anniversary of D-Day. The beach landing in Normandy was commemorated by veterans, who—if they still could—suited up and parachuted out of C-130s to the beaches. This time they were not met by caltrops, Czech hedgehogs, and gunfire but instead by cheering crowds, herds of media, and the rapid fire of camera shutters.

It was at this time that Grampa and Coco traveled to France to retrace the 134th Regiment's campaign. They went to St. Lo, a small town in Normandy. St. Lo was the site of some of the fiercest fighting of the war. It was at St. Lo that some companies would endure astronomical casualty rates as high as 180 percent. It was also where Grampa himself had been shot.

Even I got caught up in the optics of the pageantry and the self-congratulatory mood of our country at the time. After all, the Cold War had just ended, the Berlin Wall had fallen, Russia was democratizing, and the wild economic ride of the nineties was just beginning. Scholars declared that we had reached the "End of History," and that liberal democracy had triumphed . . . forever! With no other rivals on the horizon, America seemed secure in its hegemony. The Fiftieth Anniversary of D-Day was a reminder that the twentieth century was, indeed, the century of American ascendance.

We had every reason to believe the 21st century would be the same.

Young and naïve, spoiled and privileged, I couldn't really appreciate the reality of what Grampa had gone through, much less what he would have experienced during that return trip to France. It was the same for the other old veterans I met at VFW halls where I read my winning essay to men sitting under clouds of cigarette smoke. They were just graying old fat guys wearing Members Only jackets and baseball caps with regimental seals and campaign bars embroidered on the crowns. These seniors were mostly harmless to me, distant, and perhaps a bit ridiculous in their fashion choices. All seemed very, *very* dated to me. Past their prime. But I knew I owed them a debt of respect, if for no other reason than because grownups told me I did, and because my grandfather was one of them.

In time, I'd have to experience my own trauma, see people I loved die, and feel the helpless terror of a life slipping away in my own arms, a life that I was helpless to save, despite all the wanting to. I would have to suffer the subsequent crises of faith, despair, and breakdowns that followed to really understand the demons that stalked Grampa.

★

Talk of a "memoir" reached fever pitch around this time, in the mid-nineties. Grampa and his like were enjoying a level of celebrity they had not seen since returning victorious from Europe fifty years before. Families and loved ones were also recognizing that they would not have their graying elders with them forever. Requests to record and document their lives were plentiful.

But Grampa was never taken with the urge to write, like I was. Coco and my mother had to gently nag him to write things down. He did so, in longhand, on a yellow legal pad. Coco would then decipher the scrawl and type it up. Additionally, there was a local reporter/historian from Omaha who asked to sit down with Grampa and interview him. The final written account of Grampa's time in the service, while rich with impressive recall, was less than a hundred pages. Grampa titled these writings *Recollections of a GI* and announced that they, combined with the lengthy taped interviews, would represent his *magnum opus.* After that, he didn't really spend much more time working on any of it.

The festivities of the fiftieth anniversary passed. The vets grew older. Grampa's own chapter of members of the 134th disbanded. They had recognized that they had become nothing but a group of old men marking the deaths of other old men. As a country, we moved on to other fads and obsessions, other wars and scandals . . . Whitewaters and White Broncos, Gary Condits and Monica Lewinskis. Spicegirls. Backstreet Boys. Star Wars prequels.

Of course, there were hints that all was not well with the Pax Americana, that it was a reprieve, rather than a new normal. Genocides in Rwanda and the former Yugoslavia reminded us of that. The Russia of Boris Yeltsin turned out not to be a democratic dream but instead began a slide back into authoritarianism under Vladimir Putin. America's enemies refused to remain vanquished, as the toxic smoke clouds of September 11th, 2001, showed us. Suddenly, the bubble of our collective fantasy popped. Terms like "the war on terror," "asymmetrical warfare," and "terror alerts," entered our lexicon. Overnight, our safety was no longer for certain.

Turned out, history hadn't ended.

Over the next ten years, wars in Afghanistan and Iraq that we couldn't win, much less end, showed us that the US was no longer absolute. The Great Recession demonstrated just how thoroughly the economic ride of the 1990s was over. Now we hear about strategic realignments, pivots towards Asia, and American decline. The twenty-first century will belong to China, the pundits say. American power has been checked, our moral standing tarnished, even our democratic process hacked. The United States of America's place in the world is no longer inviolate. We're no longer invulnerable. We're not the big kid on the block anymore.

A bit like things were amidst the uncertainty of the 1930s and early 40s. And it's all the more daunting because, with time, we've come to realize more than ever, that even our heroes of old were imperfect.

After his death, Grampa left my mother his medals, along with the pages of his memoir and the tapes of his interviews. This was in part because she was the oldest of his children, but also because he remarked that, of all his grandchildren, I had shown the most interest and enthusiasm about his service. My years of wearing his replica jacket and the watch emblazoned with the crest of the 134th had not gone unnoticed.

But by then, approaching my forties, I harbored my own ambivalence towards the memory of my grandfather. My frustration and disappointment with Grampa had only grown after his death. This had happened as more of his grandchildren shared stories of his behavior in the last weeks and months of his life. He tripped and fell with greater frequency at family gatherings. He passed out watching college football games with an empty cup in his hand. It took more effort than usual to rouse him. At first, we had tried to explain it away, assuming his falls, his fatigue were the result of old age, his kidney surgery, low blood pressure . . . anything but alcohol.

By the end, our own denial became less and less tenable.

I saw Grampa to a limited extent in these last months. He was by turns reflective on his mortality and explosive towards minor frustrations, a side of him I had never known. It was as if the two sides of Robert Fowler, war hero and drunk, were wrestling it out before my eyes. After his death, I heard from one or two cousins similar accounts of behavior that swung wildly between extremes of the man we loved and a figure we felt embarrassment towards. The sense of disappointment grew into sorrow as we became aware that, at some point, he had lost his sobriety right under our noses. More disappointments tallied up as we compared notes. Sorrow grew to shame. So much so that when Coco passed, and Grampa's medals finally came to my mother and to me—it pains me to admit—I wasn't even sure I wanted them.

But perhaps in her own effort to try to make sense of the man her father was, my mother picked up the last pages of his memoir, the pages Coco had never gotten around to typing, and decided to finish transcribing them herself. A daughter's last gesture to know her father. Shortly after Mom finished, with help from my father, she came to me. I had finally become a published, fulltime writer. She asked me if could I make sense of the narrative, edit it into something cohesive, to make sure Grampa's story was told.

Less out of any remaining loyalty to my grandfather and more out of love for my mother, I said I would take a look. But I promised nothing.

I wasn't sure what I would think of the memoir, what it would be like to encounter Grampa in his own words. This was 2018. More than a decade had passed since his death, almost two decades since the fiftieth anniversary, almost eight decades since WWII. We were even coming up now on the seventy-fifth anniversary.

Time flies.

Since then, our country has moved on to new movements . . . new moments of crisis. We're grappling with growing economic inequality. We're reexamining gender, race, and prejudice in our country. We've grown disillusioned with wars after the ambiguous, longstanding conflicts in Afghanistan and Iraq. We are facing rising waves of nativism, shorter life expectancies, opioid and obesity epidemics, unending mass shootings, and crumbling standards of living and infrastructure. Wages are stagnant. Hate crimes are more frequent. White supremacist groups have reemerged. We are witnessing never before seen environmental degradation and climate change. Our news feeds are filled with images of intransigent violence from our police against people of color. Our trust in institutions, our security in a sense of privacy, and our faith in democracy have eroded; so have traditional norms of political discourse and governmental checks and balances. Compounding this are technologies that promised to unite us: the internet, social media, ecommerce, mobile phones. These inventions were supposed to usher in a life of convenience, connectivity, and community. It would be a new era in which we would have leisure time to pursue our higher purposes. But they have done the opposite, dividing us, isolating us, and undermining our security. The rat race has only gotten faster and more congested. A telecommuting, gig-economy has only made the turn, churn, and burn of workers more rapid.

All this while the elders warn us against the stirrings of fascism in foreign capitals—and all too close to home. Watchdog groups warn of a growing surveillance state, our own and those of our rivals. In addition to that, the prosperity that the generations before my own grew up with, that created guarantees of good jobs, good wages, of affordable homes, and the ability to live without debt, has diminished if not vanished. For young people, the overall certainty of the American experiment has fundamentally come into question, as it has not for decades.

Maybe not since the 1930s?

Amid this, my mother was asking me to go back, to sit with Grampa again. To revisit this fallen hero and find something . . . redeemable? Some of his own daughters had grown to resent him to such an extent that one dared not to mention him in their presence. My mother was asking me to go through a reexamination I feared would only end in more disappointment. It promised to be an exercise in making my communal disenchantment with generations before, with the country in general, into something specific, personal, and painful.

I wanted to leave Grampa buried.

But she is my mother, and so I said I would try. And maybe, I hoped, there might be answers, for how Grampa and his generation faced adversity, uncertainty, a threatening world. Maybe, therein, I might uncover some lessons for the uncertain times we face now.

Mom sent me the memoir, and I sat down at my laptop to read it and encounter Grampa once more. This time at my own pace, older and with a few more years of experience under my belt. I was unsure as what to expect. But the narrative would take me to the crux of the matter quickly enough. After pages delineating the training Grampa and his regiment went through in preparation for the war, I came to the second half of his story, the description of the pivotal battle for Hill 122 and St. Lo.

If you are not a history buff, it is hard to appreciate the importance of the battle for St. Lo. The charge into the German fortifications from the beaches of Normandy has become the iconic image seared into our national consciousness of the war. The casualties and courage of that struggle became emblematic of the loss and heroism of so many soldiers in the European theater.

But the landing was just the beginning. It was a foothold, won dearly, but a tenuous one. The Allies had to gain more ground in the Normandy invasion and fast, or Hitler's armies would repel them. One of the first and crucial towns to capture was St. Lo. Even though it was smaller than the neighboring city of Cherbourg, St. Lo occupied a strategic crossroads that the Allies knew they had to capture. It is no exaggeration to say that the campaign to topple the Third Reich hinged on it.

The Nazis knew this too. They knew it with the same clarity as the Allies. After D-Day, the war was hardly over. The Axis could still win. They just had to hold the town of St. Lo and the hills around it. Stop the advance before it built momentum.

The battle of St. Lo *would* be a crucial win for the Allies and the war on the western front, allowing them to eventually push deeper into France, to liberate Paris, and to drive the Germans all the way back to Berlin. It was these early battles in Normandy where German generals would actually later reflect that they had lost the war.

For the men who survived this fighting, like my grandfather, these battles were the inflection points of their lives. In hindsight, they knew that their courage in the face of terrible odds had ended the Holocaust, toppled fascism, and spread democracy. Their victory ushered in at least fifty years of American prosperity. This meant safety and affluence for their children and their children's children.

In retrospect, it seems inevitable. Especially to all of us brought up on a diet of Steven Spielberg films and Tom Hanks-produced miniseries. And yet, victory was anything but guaranteed. But long odds did not deter young American GIs from throwing their bodies into the maelstrom, risking not only their lives, but their souls. Victory would come at a cost no one would anticipate. No one had time to. The urgency had always been too great, the stakes too high.

The soul wounds these men carried from battle, like so many veterans, remained with them long after they returned home. The psychic, emotional, even spiritual wounds as bad, if not worse, than the physical ones, even today.[1] These wounds are the darker side of

---

[1] The US Veterans Administration 2016 National Suicide Data Report lists the following, sobering statistics: (1) the rate of suicide among all US veterans is 22 percent than the general population; (2) suicide rates for female veterans is 2.5 times higher than non-veteran adult women; (3) the rate of suicide among male veterans is 1.4 times higher than non-veteran adult men; (4) male veterans age 18-34 have the highest *rates* of suicide while male veterans 55 and older have the

any conflict. They remain long after the guns have gone silent. They manifest in nightmares, addictions, and startlingly high suicide rates among veterans. Today, we track these rates somewhat better than in the 1940s, but the truth the statistics reveal is horrifying: as a country we lose as many as 20 veterans a day to suicide. *There have been many years in which we have lost more veterans to suicide than combat.*

This inner turmoil would give lie to the veneer of peace and prosperity that would follow in the US after World War II. Fissures of pain would be buried beneath the confetti of victory parades, only to become fault lines in men's psyches and in their families as the years went by.

The simple end of the story, and the ultimate bottom line, is that these young men did triumph. We did win. We've flourished as a nation as a result. None of that is in doubt. But it is a bit more nuanced. There is always a shadow cast by even the brightest of lights.

St. Lo defined for Grampa and our family, his life—much in the same way World War II defined a century for our country. I knew that to understand Grampa, I had to delve into the words he had left me, study the context of the time, and read into the subtext of all he had left us in his memoir. What was before me was my own quest to try to find what was redeemable about his story—to reexamine what superficial triumph, personal faults, and family resentments had buried. I needed to find the thing that made Grampa a hero, even if a fallen one.

I had to find St. Lo.

---

highest *count*; (5) 69 percent of veteran suicide deaths result from a firearm injury; (6) 14 of the average 20 daily veteran suicides are individuals not receiving care from the VA. The full updated report is available here:
https://www.mentalhealth.va.gov/suicide_prevention/data.asp
Updated statistics and further analysis are available here:
https://www.va.gov/opa/pressrel/pressrelease.cfm?id=2951

REFLECTIONS III.
Guides
Ted Neill

I have been fortunate enough to have guides on this journey to "find" St. Lo. These have been facilitators who have accompanied me in this reexamination of Grampa and his life, providing perspective, wisdom, and insight.

The first was Professor Steve Olson. Steve Olson PhD was my boss at the Center for Ethics and Leadership at Georgia State University J. Mack Robinson School of Business. It was GSU that offered me a scholarship for my MBA in 2011. It came with a work-study position as a research and teaching assistant. Steve Olson was my boss.

To witness Steve in the classroom is to witness one of the most gifted and charismatic teachers you will ever meet in your lifetime. His office shelves are spilling over with teaching awards, and his reviews on Rate My Professor are full of superlatives—in the best way. In addition to his prodigious knowledge, his rigorous preparation, and his infectious enthusiasm, he is accessible, passionate, and a friend to all his students. He is also a deeply moral man—as one might expect from the director of the Center for Ethics.

I was blessed to have Steve as my boss and friend in 2012, when a series of life events and my own unaddressed trauma sent me spiraling into clinical depression. Suicidal and diagnosed with major depressive disorder, I had to be hospitalized. It was during this time in the hospital that I really began to examine my own scars from working and living at an orphanage for children with HIV/AIDS in Nairobi, Kenya, from 2002 to 2004. I had suppressed so much of my own pain, the lingering moral questions, and the unresolved heartbreak of seeing children I had come to love suffer and die. I had felt powerless to help in each case, and useless at improving circumstances on a wider scale. The experience had left me shattered, and yet I had tried to "soldier on" for years after.[2]

It was Steve, as much as the doctors, therapists, and fellow patients, that introduced me to a framework and vocabulary that

---

[2] These experiences are more fully explored in my memoir, *Two Years of Wonder,* all proceeds from which go back to helping the children affected by and infected with HIV/AIDS featured in its pages and others like them.

allowed me to begin to unravel the "soul wounds" that had so fractured my own identity. These were psychic injuries that, left unhealed, had come back to cripple me. Additionally, Steve allowed me to come back to my job post-hospitalization. He did this even though I was not yet a student again. Having missed too many lectures and assignments, I had to wait for the next semester to begin attending classes again. I was also on academic probation. I had failed all my classes the previous semester. It turns out that being locked in a psych ward and heavily medicated doesn't make you the best student.

Despite my ambiguous academic standing, Steve insisted I still come and even get paid my stipend. This brought structure back to my life, without too much pressure to perform. It allowed me to slowly rebuild a sense of self-respect and independence—critical after you have been on lockdown with your belt and shoelaces taken from you, where you can't even shave because you can't be trusted with a razor.

An addict in recovery once told me that, while in rehab, he burst into tears that first morning that he was clear enough to simply make his bed. For him, making that bed was the first time in years that he had been able to see a task through to completion. It was the first time he could even say to himself, "I've done a good job." For him, it was a humble cornerstone to start rebuilding a life.

Steve gave that same opportunity to me. He gave me the space, opportunity, and most of all, the love that allowed me to begin a process of catharsis, meaning finding, and healing. He would introduce me to authors and speakers who would inform my journey. He was also constantly receptive and open to simply discussing my healing process, never once uncomfortable with the messiness and uncertainty of the recovery process. He was never afraid to witness another person's pain or sit with the raw vulnerability of a grown man.

I would later learn that he had learned to do this through his own work alongside veterans.

It was through Steve that I met my next guide, Jack Hoban. Jack is a retired Marine Corps captain. In addition to being an instructor on martial arts, combat ethics, and conflict resolution, Jack

Hoban is the author of a number of books, including *The Ethical Warrior* and *The Ethical Protector.*[3]

Jack Hoban's mentor throughout his career was Robert L. Humphrey, PhD. Humphrey was a world-renowned conflict resolution specialist. It was Humphrey who introduced Jack to the *Life Value Theory* (also known as the *Dual Life Value Theory*). Jack has been one the most important advocates for the *Life Value Theory* after Humphrey's death.

Essentially, the core of the *Life Value Theory* is that all life is sacred, even the life of the (supposed) enemy. The *Dual Life Value Theory* has revolutionized approaches to conflict resolution, combat, and combat training for the US armed forces, police departments, even non-profits and business leaders world-wide. It hinges not on the soldier or police officer identifying with the role of aggressor but rather as *protector*—a protector of life. Yes, they may have to take life in the course of their duties, but it is only a last resort and only if in service of protecting life.

Steve Olson met Jack Hoban through the consulting work Steve was doing in Quantico, Virginia. At Quantico, an innovative program was exposing civilian leaders to Marine Corps ethics training. Executives from the profit and non-profit sectors would be dropped into simulated combat settings in wilderness and urban environments. They would be exposed to the mental hardships and physical exhaustion of combat—diminished sleep, rations, and long marches. The trainees would be equipped with guns loaded with blanks and exposed to explosive devices modified to produce all the shock and noise of real artillery—without the casualties. They would have to achieve a number of mission objectives while being faced with a series of ethical dilemmas that would be facilitated (and often complicated) by role players—veterans themselves who had real-life experience of the very dilemmas presented in each simulation. By design, the scenarios would pit one moral principle against another and push the trainees to the point of failure, which was where the best learning took place.[4] The trainings, through their rigor, helped to clarify moral

---

[3] Full Titles: *The Ethical Warrior: Values, Morals and Ethics; The Ethical Protector: Police Ethics, Tactics and Techniques.*

[4] These dilemmas were based on the five in the Moral Foundations Theory, as articulated by Jonathan Haidt, PhD. The five principles are: (1) *Care*—cherishing and protecting others; the opposite of harm. (2) *Fairness or proportionality*—rendering justice according to shared rules; the opposite of cheating. (3)

imperatives. Post-training, participants universally reported improved ability to communicate ethical priorities and make decisions, even under pressure. After all, the boardroom is a serene setting in comparison to combat.

In 2010, after a particularly difficult training scenario, as a first-time consultant in the program, Steve Olson led a debriefing exercise with a number of participants from the private sector who had failed, *spectacularly,* to accomplish their mission objectives—much less uphold moral precepts. Steve was able to revisit the scenario with the shamefaced participants, reexamining the opposing ethical priorities and resulting breakdowns with such clarity that the supervising Marine officers were gob smacked. Their initial reaction was enthusiastic, but (these being Marines) mainly unprintable in polite company.

Needless to say, Steve was invited back, not only to work with business leaders but members of all four branches of the services.

That was when he crossed paths with Jack Hoban himself, who was working to introduce the *Dual Life Value Theory* into combat training for Marines.

Jack is a warrior and teacher in the deepest, most spiritual of senses. He and Steve struck up a natural friendship, and Steve introduced me to Jack in the months after I left the hospital. I was in the process of rebuilding my life, and Steve thought it might be beneficial for me to sit down with Jack. Jack, in a single one-on-one meeting with me, graciously drew parallels between my own experiences witnessing children's deaths in Kenya and those of the battlefield.[5] While I'd never claim to have endured the same ordeals

---

Loyalty or ingroup—standing with your group, family, nation; the opposite of betrayal. (4) *Authority or respect*—submitting to tradition and legitimate authority; the opposite of subversion. (5) *Sanctity or purity:* abhorrence for disgusting things, foods, actions, pollution; opposite of degradation/profane. Haidt is also developing a sixth category (6) *Liberty,* as the freedom from oppression and coercion.

[5] While I remain skeptical of any one worldview as providing *all* the answers, between the *Dual Life Value Theory* and the precepts of what I was learning through my friends in Alcoholics Anonymous (whom I had met in treatment and rehab at the psychiatric hospital), I felt like I had stumbled upon grounded, moral frameworks that were more informed by real life and more practical than anything I had encountered in organized religion. In time, both would become invaluable to me.

that military veterans must survive, Jack's acknowledgment of the long shadow mourning can cast, his introduction to psychic versus moral injury, the identities of protector, and the archetype of the warrior, provided me a roadmap for my own journey and eventual healing.[6]

It would also lay the groundwork for an understanding of Robert Lewis Fowler.

It was Steve and Jack who introduced me to the scholarship of Edward Tick, PhD. Edward Tick is a psychotherapist with over forty years of experience working with veterans. He has become a well-known expert on the effects of war and the process of reconciliation and restoration. Tick's process is informed by medicine, psychology, and spirituality. Although I have never met Dr. Tick in person, his books *War and the Soul* and *Warrior's Return: Restoring the Soul After War* gave me better insight into the particular experience of the individual soldier and the unique wounds war leaves on the soul.

Tick views war as a mythical construct. War itself is an archetype, and it has a deep, inexplicable pull on us. So much a pull that war shows up in even our most sacred texts. This is universal from one culture to the next. The Bible is no exception to this truth, even the New Testament, which despite its emphasis on the importance of "loving thy neighbor" and "turning the other cheek," still ends with the epic battle between good and evil as depicted in the book of Revelation.

This is a reminder, Tick points out, of the undeniable pull of war and violence on our souls. It is for that very reason that war can shatter more than our bodies, but our souls too. It's pull on us borders

---

[6] While many of these roles, such as protector and warrior, have been traditionally male, I've purposefully chosen not to attribute them solely to masculinity. Partly this is in acknowledgement of the many women now serving in these roles in the armed forces and as police officers. But also because, increasingly, I believe the traits that make a good man are truly the same traits that make a good woman; positive attributes, I believe, should be open to all people, no matter which socially constructed gender they might be traditionally associated with. The discussion of what makes a good man or a good woman today is less and less relevant as we recognize these are socially constructed constructs. The virtues that make us good, moral humans belong equally to all people regardless of gender.

on the supernatural. Tick argues that post-traumatic stress is best understood not in terms of a stress disorder but, rather, an identity disorder, a moral trauma that has caused a wound to the soul. This would show up in veterans of even "good" and "just" wars such as World War II, where men went away to "save humanity" but returned feeling like mass murderers.[7]

It is for this reason that Jack Hoban's reorientation of soldiers not as trained killers, but protectors of life (even the enemy's life!), has been so transformational in military training and effective at reducing rates of post-traumatic stress. As mentioned before, this orientation is what gave me further insight into my time working the hospice for children dying of AIDS and the post-traumatic stress I experienced afterwards. Faced with the reality of powerlessness in trying to alleviate the suffering of children, my own sense of self had been fractured. I had gone to help, only to realize I was helpless. I grew close to the children, only to eventually abandon them myself. These were contradictions in my identity I could not resolve on my own.

Tick shares that in traditional societies, the journey to war, the encounter with violence and mortality, the return to society, and the subsequent healing and reintegration was a process facilitated by elders and community. It was carefully choreographed and managed through rituals and mentorship to stitch back together the wounds trauma left. Leaving for war, and returning from war, was an ancient, elaborate, and refined rite of passage.

For many soldiers in the 1940s and sadly up to the present day, this process has been completely lacking. Our process of reintegration has been insufficient to address the spiritual and psychological wounds inflicted by battle. Returning veterans often become isolated from mainstream society. Many turn to drugs, alcohol, vandalism, promiscuity, and other risky behaviors. These serve as incomplete and inadequate replacements for passages and rites that were once managed lovingly by wise elders. This leads to further complications among veterans such as domestic violence, compounding mental health disorders, and, in too many cases, suicide. This has been, and is, and underreported tragedy, as one recent study of Afghanistan and Iraqi War veterans found 13.9 percent suffering from post-traumatic

---

[7] Tick, Edward. *War and the Soul.* Quest Books, 2012.

stress, 39 percent qualifying for probable alcohol abuse and 3 percent for drug abuse.[8]

Slowly, after reading Tick, I was beginning to comprehend what battles had followed Grampa home and the demons he faced throughout his life, even up to his death. I had even begun to see parallels between his journey and my own.

My final and most unexpected guide was Gordon Edward Cross. I came across his *Diary of a Front Line Medic* while researching documents on the 134th Infantry Division website. I've written more on the process of discovering his own harrowing memoir and the experience of reading it for the first time in the coming pages dedicated to Cross. It's enough to say here that his account provided a perspective on the chaos, carnage, and courage of the battlefield that even my grandfather's memoir had not. I'm indebted to his son, William G. Cross (Bill) for making it available and sharing it here. It opened my eyes further to the ordeal of combat, from the gritty details to the emotional toll. I hope it does the same for you.

But that is enough from me. It's about time I turned the wheel over to Grampa and Gordon.

---

[8] Susan V. Eisen et al. "Mental and Physical Health Status and Alcohol and Drug Use Following Return From Deployment to Iraq or Afghanistan", *American Journal of Public Health* 102, no. S1 (March 1, 2012): pp. S66-S73.

RECOLLECTIONS OF A GI
I.
Robert Lewis Fowler

Nebraska, 1937 — Signing Up

My military experience started on July 22nd, 1937.

I was sixteen years old when my mother told me about a friend who knew a person I could contact to earn thirty dollars in fifteen days. In 1937 that was a substantial amount of money.

That person was a window-dresser at Kresge's store, 16th & Harney streets, Omaha. His name was Albert Osborne, and I was contacted on the job. He told me to ask for him—Sergeant Osborne—the following Monday night at 7:00 PM at the National Guard Armory, 12th & Dodge streets.

I followed instructions, and after finding him, he took me to the office, later known as the orderly room, and I filled out a job application that turned into enlistment papers in the Nebraska National Guard. During this process a big mean-looking guy in uniform came by and says "You sure don't look eighteen." I had been told I had to lie about my age and that it didn't matter, so I bluffed it out. Later, I found out the guy was First Sergeant Burmeister, and he was the "Big Boss." He had some funny-looking patches on each sleeve, and I found out later they were his insignia of rank. He was also boss of all the other sergeants and corporals and everybody but the officers.

The deal was that we were to come to the Armory for two hours every Monday evening and, as a private, we would receive one dollar, payable in cash every three months. Also, once a year we would go to summer camp for two weeks and we would get a dollar a day from the US Government and a dollar a day from the State of Nebraska. Since we were scheduled to go to Camp Funston, Kansas, for our summer camp the first two weeks of August, we were to be on duty fifteen days. Thereafter we would receive a total of thirty dollars for doing what we were told, later was known to be "playing soldier." I also found out I had signed up to do this routine for three years. The thirty dollars I would receive in August I needed for my senior year in High School; the twelve dollars quarterly pay came in very handy also.

After filling out my enlistment papers I was given a uniform and some help in putting it on: one wool OD (olive drab) shirt, black string tie, khaki breeches, belt, GI high-top shoes, and a campaign hat. I also received two rolls of OD wool strip material about three inches wide and five or six feet long with a funny little cotton tab or tape on one end. I was now the proud owner of a pair of wrap leggings. Since our trousers were breeches, the leggings were wrapped top to bottom, starting approximately four inches below the knee, and spiraled downward to around the ankle and top of the shoe. I was told the mark of a good soldier was how well he could wrap his leggings, and woe be unto the goofball whose leggings came unwrapped during drill or in formation. Needless to say, this became my first military accomplishment, and I was proud of myself.

The most important issue item was a 1903 Springfield rifle. It was clip fed, .30-millimeter caliber, with five rounds per clip, one bayonet to fit said rifle, and a cartridge belt that would hold about twenty-five-round clips. The rifle became my "piece," and it had a number which was to be memorized for life (which I have forgotten); we were not yet burdened with a serial number, 20723530 (which I have not). The weapon was never referred to after that as a rifle or a gun. Rifles were for civilians and guns were for artillery. At this time, all items of issue were stored in individual bins in the supply room and were used only during drill. Of course, you came to drill early enough to put on the uniform and be able to "fall in" formation when called by the First Sergeant.

My first drill after the first "fall in" consisted of rookie instruction, later to be known as basic training. This included wearing of the uniform, military courtesy, manual of arms, and close order drill. At this time, the uniforms and the style of close order drill were all World War I vintage, which was squads left or right and right front into line.

My instructor was PFC (private first class) Kenneth Gidley, who later would be Corporal Gidley, my squad leader, and three years later he would be the person whose stripes I would receive at the time I became a squad leader corporal.

During my rookie training I was informed the company commander was Captain Al Thompson, the executive officer was First Lieutenant Earl H. Kelso, and the platoon leader was First Lieutenant Hall. These were the people I had to salute and call "Sir," along with every other officer like them, regardless of what unit or branch of service.

I also found out that I was in the first squad of the second platoon of Company "L"—134th Infantry Regiment of the 69th Brigade of the 35th Division. The Division also included National Guard troops from Missouri and Kansas as well as Nebraska.

Kansas: Camp Funston, 1937

August 1937 came along as a big adventure. By this time, I knew how to put on my uniform, wrap my leggings, do the manual of arms, and to whom to say "Sir" and how to salute the same. The trip to Camp Funston (next to Fort Riley, Kansas) was via passenger train, and the vintage of the train cars had to be pre-1900. We were pretty dirty by the time we arrived.

We were billeted in five-man pyramidal tents with canvas army cots with mattress covers we filled with straw. We had been issued two wool blankets and a set of blue dungarees, which were to be worn on work details.

Each company had enough tents for its troops (approx. ninety men). Tents extended east from the orderly room tent as did all the other companies in the regiment. Temporary sheds with showers and latrine facilities, one per company, at the end of each row. There was no mess hall. Chow was served from a mess tent by Gibby (Clinton Gibson), the mess sergeant, and his crew. I found he cooked a lot better when he had a proper amount of bourbon and seemed to get by with it, since he could do wonders with Government-issue food. I found out later that he had been a chef on the Union Pacific Streamliners, so he had plenty of experience in his trade. I learned that Captain Thompson was a blacksmith for the UP Shops. He was big enough for the job. He also seemed to be a real nice guy. Little did I know then the associations I would have with him in the future.

The purpose we were in Kansas for our summer camp was for maneuvers involving several divisions of troops, and we were in the field and sleeping on the ground most of the time we were there. The middle Saturday was known as Governor's Day and required a great parade of all troops. It was long and dusty and very hot. Temperatures ran into low 90 degrees in the daytime, and there was very little shade anywhere. The parade was probably the most disagreeable experience of the entire two weeks. Payday was the second Saturday. After that, trips to the canteen tent for 3.2 beer with the big boys were a great experience, even though the beer didn't taste any better than my father's home brew, which I never did like. That evening we broke camp and located our gear on trains for the trip home. The puffed up feeling of a great experience had most of us rookies keyed up and anxious to get home and tell everyone about our great accomplishments.

During the time we were in the cantonment area of the summer camp there were certain bugle calls at different times of the day, and of course this was part of a rookie's education to learn what was going on. At Reveille—approximately six AM—everyone "falls in" to his proper place in a company front formation, and the squad leaders report on the presence of their men to the platoon sergeant, who reports to the first sergeant, and the first sergeant, in turn, gives the total report to the company commander, who gives the command "POSTS," at which time the first sergeant and the platoon sergeant move to a position in back of the platoons, and the officers come forward in front of their platoons, facing the company commander. This procedure is done each time the company is formed during the day. Call for drill was after breakfast and again after dinner.

At 5:00 or 5:30 PM, is the most important formation of the day: Retreat. The company forms in the usual manner. Normally, the best and cleanest uniform is worn; it is always specified by the first sergeant. At this formation the usual reports are taken and announcements made, but the main reason for being there is to pay allegiance to the National Colors. All companies are called to attention and the command "Present Arms" is given. During this time, either the bugler plays the call "To the Colors" over the loud speaker system so that all companies hear it or the Regimental Band plays the National Anthem. In either case, at the end of the music, a cannon fires and the Flag is lowered and folded properly by the sergeant of the guard. The command "Order Arms" is given. The ceremony is over, and the units dismissed. Chow call comes next and, of course, taps later, around 9:00 or 9:30 PM.

It was while attending my first "Retreat" ceremony formation as the band played the National Anthem that I felt a tingling up my spine and a pride in membership that I have never forgotten. I still experience that tingling feeling under similar circumstances and probably always will.

Up until that first Retreat ceremony, I had read many books and seen a few movies that dealt with patriotism, and I felt that it was an important part of being a citizen of the

USA. But that first experience placed things into perspective for me so that I was able to handle the difficult and undesirable experiences of future military activities.

After the first summer camp, the weekly drills started to become more comprehensible because of the short period of rookie training before summer camp. Things that happened during camp were making more sense.

I found out that the National Guard wore two hats. Normally the Guard is under state control and is available to the governor for riot control duty, disaster assistance, and anti-looting protection. When normal local police protection is overwhelmed, the governor can employ the National Guard upon request by the mayor of the community involved.

To begin with, the Minute Men of pre-Revolutionary War days were the original National Guard, making it the first military units of the country. The National Guard can be called up by the president for war time duty through an act of Congress. This has been done many times in the past.

I began to feel that I was doing something besides earning a few dollars for school expenses.

Normally, everyone in the outfit had to qualify with his assigned weapon each year. Due to lack of time and adequate facilities, weapon firing could not be accomplished at summer camp. I started to receive instruction in firing the 03, and this was the most interesting part of training for me. I had always liked to shoot and had done quite a bit of hunting and shooting .22s and had some knack for the activity. Many hours of practice or "dry firing" are spent before a person actually fires on the range. Use of the sling for steadying the "piece" was new to me. Numerous positions such as prone, sitting, kneeling and standing, and slow fire then rapid fire gradually became familiar.

Nebraska: Camp Ashland, 1938

Summer camp 1938 was at Ashland, Nebraska, where all the units in the state assembled. Twenty companies of the 134th Infantry Regiment plus 110 Medics, 110 Quartermasters and one Battalion of Artillery, some engineers, and other support type units all made up the Nebraska National Guard.

Actual firing on the range was a great experience, and I did well for a rookie. There are three qualification categories: Marksman, Sharpshooter and Expert. I made sharpshooter the first year. I made expert the next year and every time after that. I never lost my enjoyment of this special skill.

After my first summer camp at Fort Riley, my enthusiasm easily sold my best friend, Leo Samson, on the idea of joining up. We had been best buddies since the spring of 1934, and where you found one of us, you found the other.

Photo Next Page: Fowler pictured front row, third from right with Leo Samson on his left.

Nebraska: Camp Ashland, 1939

In 1939, we again went to Ashland for our summer camp, and we did the same type of training we had been doing in the past. However, in the ensuing months war had started in Europe and things seemed to get a little more serious. The week before Christmas and New Year's was spent on duty at old Fort Crook. It was then the home of the Regular Army, 17th Infantry. It later became Offutt Air Force Base and Sac Command Headquarters. Our time there was spent in indoor classrooms and on a miniature indoor firing range using .22 rifles built on 03 "chassis". We fired at paper "picture type" terrain targets and fired as squads, using the old "musketry" theory of controlled fire by the squad leader. It was advanced type training for us.

Sometime during 1939 I received my first stripe. I became a PFC and assistant squad leader. Pay went from $1.00 per drill or day to

$1.15. It took over two years to make that jump in rank.

Minnesota: Camp Ripley, 1940

1940 brought extra drills. We were encouraged to request the correspondence course from Fort Benning, known then as "Ten Series". Up until this time, you had to be a sergeant in order to request it, but now we all were encouraged to take it as a means of furthering our military education. This was also a means of obtaining an "M" Day Commission as a second lieutenant any time the outfit was mobilized into active federal service.

Many of us applied for the series. It was controlled and graded by the Infantry Officers School at Fort Benning and normally took well over a year to complete. It did provide an extra source of training and information that benefited us all later. Prior to summer camp 1940, I had completed the first series of the "Ten Series" and taken the test and passed it. Next there was a test given by our own officers for future promotion, as a reward for the higher scores. Thanks to the "Ten Series" from Benning, I came out in pretty good shape.

That year we went to summer camp in the vicinity of Camp Ripley, Minnesota. We were located at the southern tip of Lake Mille Lacs. We were there for three weeks instead of the usual two due to the war situation. The draft was ready to start September 16, 1940. The law that was passed to start the draft called for one year of military training for all able-bodied male citizens of the United States. It also automatically mobilized all reserve components of the military as soon as facilities became available. There were rumors we would not return home from camp but would proceed to our new post, wherever that might be.

After being in summer camp for a little over a week, I learned that Corporal Gidley, my squad leader and the person that gave me my first training, was being demoted. I never knew why. I always liked him and thought he was an OK corporal. Because of his misfortune, I became a corporal. I immediately wondered if I had studied enough.

Captain Thompson had been assigned to Regimental Headquarters as adjutant. First Lieutenant Earl Kelso became captain and company commander of L Company. First Lieutenant Wallace B. Hall became executive officer, and Sergeant Albert Osborne became Lieutenant Osborne. I had long since learned not to mention who had recruited me. Osborne was not very well thought of by the men and even his fellow officers, but completing the Ten Series really paid off for him. I returned with the company to Omaha as corporal and squad leader of Third Squad, Second Platoon, Company L.

We were told we did not need draft cards. Our National Guard membership was all we needed, since we knew by then we would be sent to Camp Joseph T. Robinson, Arkansas, as soon as the camp was ready to receive us.

We were allowed ninety-six men max in a rifle company at that time, and we had a waiting list of people who wanted to join. The Guard had always been a volunteer outfit. The members who were married were allowed to be discharged if they wanted to be. There were plenty who wanted in, so there were no problems. Those that were discharged were older married men, mostly sergeants who could not afford to support a family on army pay. This did make way for some new promotions, and I think that was when my buddy, Leo Samson, made corporal. My brother Jim Fowler joined up, even though he was as young then as I had been when I joined. We still had our weekly drills and some extras sometimes on Saturday and Sunday.

REFLECTIONS IV.
Nebraska, Summer 1995
Ted Neill

The summer before my senior year in high school Grampa took me on a car trip across his home state of Nebraska. He set a Stetson cowboy hat on my head with a 134th Regiment pin on the crown that matched his own, and we set off in his powder blue Lincoln Town Car. It was set with all the luxury extras of the day: leather seats, power windows, interior wood accents, and a digital dash display. He told me how he had worked out a long-term lease on the car that, for an old man like himself, was more advantageous than buying it. I remember finding it touching, the pride he showed in having his finances in order so that there actually would be a "few thousand dollars" to leave behind to his surviving daughters. It was a modest amount. But for a man who had been unable to provide for his children's most basic needs growing up, being able to leave behind any inheritance whatsoever was a joy to him.

Photo: Fowler and Neill at the beginning of their trip, summer 1995.

That first morning we drove south along Interstate 29, down into Iowa. We were tracking along the Missouri River. Grampa pointed out a few of the quirks in geography that had come from the Missouri flooding and rearranging the banks, leaving bits of Nebraska "stranded" to the east of the river and bits of Iowa to the west.

We continued south into the state of Missouri. About an hour out of Omaha we reached the town of Tarkio. Throughout Grampa's lifetime the town's population hovered around 2,500.[9] But even in 1995 it was a town so small that I only remember a few dozen buildings spread about. We only stopped at one: the home where Grampa was born. It was a house on the roadside set on the rolling crest of a hill, with a cemetery not too far away where my ancestors were buried—ancestors only Grampa had known in life and I never would.

Photo: Neill next to the gravestone of his great-great-great-grandparents, Thomas Fowler and his wife Rachel.

---

[9] Today, the population is about half that, the lowest it has been since 1900.

Grampa's childhood home was constructed in the simple foursquare "prairie box" style of homes built in the late 1800s and early 1900s. The yard was without trees for windbreaks. The house itself lacked any architectural flourishes. Instead, it possessed all the middle-of-the-plains simplicity that must have been all the starker amid the dust bowl years of the Great Depression.

Grampa was born in this house April 24, 1921, the doctor arriving to deliver him in a horse-drawn carriage. Grampa's mother had always told him he had been born in the middle of a blizzard. He admitted to me he always had trouble believing this and speculated that his mother had confused the context of his birth with that of one of his four siblings. At least he had until that very year, 1995, when Omaha was struck with a spring snowstorm that left several inches on the ground on his seventy-fourth birthday. He had taken a photo to document it and showed it to me. "Never really believed it until I saw it for myself," he said, then let out an understated chuckle characteristic of him—just the barest of commentary. Grampa never needed you to think a certain way or to arrive at a specific opinion that aligned with his own. He never hung on your reaction. He just presented a story, a photograph, a fact, for your review. You were allowed to come to your own conclusions. It made for good company—he didn't need you to be anyone but yourself.

From Tarkio we headed back north, veering back into Nebraska on Route 2 while we were still well south of Omaha. This took us due west, past Lincoln. We didn't stop, but passing close to the city, it was not hard to see the designated historical landmark of the Nebraska State Capitol building. The building, constructed of Indiana limestone over the course of a decade from 1922 to 1932, is home to the country's only unicameral state legislature. It also houses the governor's office, the Supreme Court, and the Court of Appeals. Designed by Bertram Grosvenor Goodhue, it was the first state capital in the US to incorporate a tower in its design. The building came to be known as the Tower of the Prairie. Its features were at once grounded in the grandeur of a gothic revivalist style of the early twentieth century, while also evocative of the distant skyscrapers of Manhattan—those symbols of the growing American optimism ushered in by a century of westward expansion and the galloping economy of the "roaring twenties."

But on the flat, near-featureless grasslands of Nebraska where the capital was constructed, without any other tall buildings to accompany the Tower of the Prairie, the folly of the design was immediately apparent to me even before Grampa shook his head as we passed. His expression was a mix of amusement and resignation—one I would see again and again amongst midwestern folk when considering the foolishness of "city folk." He told me how most Nebraskans he knew referred to the capital building, with its narrow shaft and domed tip, as the "Penis of the Prairie," a nickname capturing their disdain for grandiose architecture and grandstanding politicians at once.

Once you "see it" as such, you can't "un-see it." At 400 feet tall and the only large building for hundreds of miles, the penis hovered in our review mirror for over 20 miles.

We continued west, stopping overnight at Grand Island and staying with some old friends of Grampa, Jack and Paula. Jack and Paula owned a ranch with a dozen Paso Fino horses. They were a husband and wife of Grampa's age, whose medium-sized stature seemed suited for the medium-sized horses. With their unique gait, Paso Finos are prized by sophisticated dressage riders as well as trail riders who favor the smoothness of the horses' trot. It has little up and down motion, even at a gallop.

Photo: Neill with some of the Paso Fino horses outside Grand Island.

At dinner we sat around the kitchen table, where Jack and Paula had a Bose Acoustic Wave Machine—a miniaturized "speaker-less" stereo marketed on AM radio stations in the 1990s. I showed some interest in it, as my mother (like Jack and Paula) had been convinced to buy one by none other than Paul Harvey, the legendary news broadcaster.

Harvey served in the US Army Air Corps in the 1940s. He had started his career broadcasting out of Chicago with the post-war employment program *Jobs for GI Joe.* Harvey represented to so many Americans in the second half of the century all that was good, wholesome, and unique to the Midwest. His *Paul Harvey News and Comment* and *Rest of the Story* broadcasts were staples on American radio for over fifty years. As a teen, even I would change over from my rock-saturated FM stations to the AM dial to hear them.

Harvey was the living embodiment of a Norman Rockwell painting. He was an authentic vestige of a midwestern and American way of being that was quickly receding into history. The only other nationally syndicated radio program to visit this ground was Garrison Keillor's *Prairie Home Companion.* But *Prairie Home Companion* was featured on Public Radio and thus tainted by its association with the espresso-drinking, tote-bag-swinging, urban yuppies set. And Keillor's nostalgic portrayals of Lake Wobegon, a town "Where all the women are strong, all the men are good looking, and all the children are above average," could come off as a winking performance, even parody, rather than something authentic.

Paul Harvey was authentic. Mother loved him and whatever he hawked, she bought. This included a Bose Wave Machine and a Buick LeSabre. But like Jack and Paula, Mom had come to find the Bose to be prone to breaking and inferior in quality (the Buick for that matter, too). Jack and Paula regarded the Wave Machine—about the size of a microwave oven—with undisguised regret and spoke of it as if they had been swindled. But there was still an element of self-doubt to their tone, bred from their trust in Paul Harvey as a pitchman. I sensed a disbelief on their parts that this trusted midwestern man, whom they had grown up with, whose voice broadcast from that one redeemable big city, Chicago (since it was in the Midwest), that he of all people would shill an inferior product for American companies that were less than world class.

In retrospect, I recognize even then, in the 1990s, some of the hairline fractures that would widen into the cultural fissures of today.

As the Federal Communications Commission rolled back the Fairness Doctrine in 1987, the stage was set for the culture and media wars of the following decades—the opening salvos thrown by the likes of Rush Limbaugh and other conservative radio hosts. In the coming years, of the Clinton, W. Bush, and Obama administrations, the fissures turned into fault lines that have become harder and harder to straddle.

In the Iraq war years of the early 2000s, even Paul Harvey picked sides. He supported the invasion of Iraq, decried welfare cheats, shamed indulgent parents, and mourned what he saw as a decline of personal responsibility and a rising culture of victimhood. "Good" people and "honest" politicians, who advocated for the rugged individualism and personal initiative that had made America successful, were losing out to "liberal" politicians on the left whose policies were leading to moral decay. Harvey's sentiments all but echoed those of firebrands and provocateurs like Limbaugh, different only in that they were delivered in that same, trustworthy, disarming midwestern drawl.

As I reached college age (Georgetown University Class of 2000), I remember reading the frustration and sense of betrayal in my mother's face as she would flip the station when Harvey came on. Especially in the last years before his death in 2009. I sensed her anger too. The characteristics she still valued—initiative, independence, hard work and perseverance, an appreciation for simplicity and common neighborly decency—midwestern principles—were being highjacked, treated as if they were the proprietary intellectual property of an increasingly conservative, nativist political movement that decried "secular," "church-hating," "God-denying," liberals. She didn't want to be a part of it. Mom wasn't secular. It was in church that she had learned compassion for the poor, the imprisoned, and the immigrant. She may have thought women should be allowed to be Catholic priests, but she certainly was not church-hating or God-denying. Even to this day she attends Mass every Sunday, where she sings in the choir. On weekdays she cantors for funerals. She's a fixture in her local parish.

But those shifts of the American political landscape have only widened since, the fissures growing into chasms as sections of the country continue to grow distant. Even Garrison Keillor fell into disgrace in the recent changing climate of #MeToo.

Keillor had always, in that gentle aw-shucks humor of his, pushed back against the rising tide of cultural change that was reexamining gender discrimination and sexism in the 1990s and into the 2000s. He was against bans on "sexualized talk" in the work place. This was oppression of speech, an overreaction to "harmless flirting," he claimed. But in the light of #MeToo and #TimesUp, what was harmless and homespun was revealed to be its own form of chauvinism. What was acceptable in the 1950s, isn't today.

When accusations of inappropriate sexual comments and even touching that Keillor had dismissed as "jokes" and "flirting" came to light, he was dropped from the show he created. It turned out that Keillor was a dinosaur, and his expiration date had passed.

I certainly endorse putting racists and sexists in their place—without a doubt and wholeheartedly. The recent emphasis on the voices of previously marginalized women, people of color, and other marginalized groups in our country is long overdue. But I also recognize we run a risk of losing a middle ground (or even common ground) as certain traits and values are ascribed to people of one background and not another. The political tactic of divide-and-conquer-through-wedge-issues, issues refined by political strategists through polling and partisan focus groups, has filtered into our culture wars and personal identities. Instead of being united by those ideals we used to consider "American," e.g. freedom of speech, of the press, of faith, equal access to opportunity and protections of the law, *the pursuit of life, liberty, and happiness,* we find ourselves defined by demographic and geographic profiles. This has only further isolated us from one another in mutual distrust, misunderstanding, and animosity.

I see the pain of this in my mother. She finds herself disoriented as she sits stranded between the political left, which presents itself as progressive and humane but increasingly doubles down on ingroup identity over a civic one; and the right, some members of which would have you think patriotism and pride of country belong to them alone—attitudes that increasingly cluster amongst the towns of Mom's midwestern home. These were the types of small towns, across the US, that men like her father came from to go to Europe in the 1940s to fight fascism, to liberate people from concentration camps, to stop regimes that stoked hatred and violence. Now she sees their children and grandchildren vote for a political party that condones the types of behaviors and beliefs their fathers fought against to stop.

Mom doesn't understand it. At times, I don't either.

But the polarization and xenophobia that plague us today felt lightyears distant that evening, sitting around the table with Grampa and his friends. Jack and Paula spoke of their horses' origins in Puerto Rico and Colombia and how much they had loved going to those places, where I imagined they must have seemed like fish-out-of-water—sunburned Anglo-Americans in jean shorts and flannel shirts with the sleeves cut off. But Jack and Paula expressed nothing but a sense of affection for the people they had met who had made them feel so welcome.

As a couple, Jack and Paula were soft spoken and slow talkers, like Grampa. Long pauses took place in the conversation, but that appeared to bother no one. I listened quietly, recognizing the extent to which Grampa was actually "bursting" with pride when he stated flatly, as if sharing a fact about the weather, that my mother was a professor of nursing and a researcher at Georgetown University.

"Well, isn't that a thing!" Paula said.

"I've right heard of that school," Jack said, nodding with approval.

In their own understated way, Jack and Paula were gushing too. My mother, the hometown girl "done good," who made it big in the distant East Coast city. A win for her was a win for all of them. She was, and always would be, one of them.

Rolling across the prairie, Grampa was in his element. Riding with him was much like riding with my mother. She and I could enjoy long silences of saying nothing. Enough was communicated in the simple sharing of the scenery, the song on the radio, or just the experience of sharing time and space together. This was something my city-slicker father could never master. On long drives, he couldn't help filling up the silence with words—mostly unneeded. It said more about his own discomfort with silence than anything else.

On dusty backroads, where walls of grass would push up against the doors of the Town Car, we passed farmers driving late model pickup trucks. All Fords and Chevys, rarely imports. The drivers would give a "country wave" as they passed: a lift of an index finger from the steering wheel. Grampa would return it in kind. There were no smiles, not even a tip of the hat or nod of the head. Those would have been wasteful, superfluous . . . a violation of the prairie minimalism, where often the only thing taller than the grass on the horizon was the occasional windmill pumping water, telephone lines that carried one, at most two, cables from pole to pole, or the occasional water tower with the town's name painted in tall letters on its side.

With the Lincoln's smooth ride and long flat stretches of road, it was easy to break the speed limit. On the one occasion that Grampa got pulled over for speeding, the "Smokey" (as Grampa called the State Trooper for his hat) took one look at the 35th Division sticker on the Town Car's bumper and put away his ticket book. He tipped his hat and, before returning to his cruiser, said, "Sorry to bother you, sir. Thank you for your service. Have a good day."

We continued west and reached Ogallala, where we stayed at the home of Grampa's childhood friend, Leo Samson. I had seen Leo in regimental photos countless times, sitting next to Grampa, his face rounder and frame stockier than Grampa's, who had always been more angular and leaner. In their seventies, both men had softened and lost their sharp edges, but I recognized Leo immediately.

Leo was jovial and friendly. He lived alone in a one-story rambler with a covered garage, his wife having passed a few years prior. Leo had a caretaker, a thirty-something woman with a nursing background, who came by daily to check on him, do a bit of cleaning, and help him on his crosswords. She was Swedish by descent, and so Leo referred to her affectionately as his "Swedish Gal," although aside from her blond hair, which was big from curlers and blow drying, she looked more classically midwestern to me than Swedish.

Ogallala is representative of many western Nebraska towns. The surrounding landscape, bereft of geographic features such as mountains or forests, possesses a grandeur that is hard to describe. The prairie is fecund with assorted fauna. We saw meadow larks, bobcats, and private herds of bison. But the prairie is also desolate, characterized by long, unbroken stretches of emptiness. Standing amid the grasslands or cornfields really is akin to being a castaway on the open sea, the occasional farm and its grain silos the only archipelagos of civilization. The landscape is complemented well by the blue-white sky, stretching from horizon to horizon during the day. Still, the nighttime sky feels like an even better match, as if only the arcing arms of the galaxy could be true companions to those long, vast spaces between towns.

The self is diminished in the face of such scales. The individual faces an existential sense of insignificance. As an antidote, the residents of rural Nebraska create features to break the monotony, then name them with a defiant sense of pomp.

With either coast thousands of miles away, the people of western Nebraska made their own ocean. They tamed the North Platte River with the Kingsley Dam to create the McConaughy Reservoir on one side and Lake Ogallala on the other. Visitors there can see the incongruous sight of jet skis, parasailing, and kite surfing against a backdrop of cottonwood trees and corn fields. Children can build sandcastles or jump into miniature breakers. It's all the charm of the ocean, right in the middle of the prairie.

No real islands? No problem; the Wood River and Platte River enclosed a small area of woodland which early French traders named *La Grande Isle.* The name was later Anglicized to Grand Island. Now the area is home to a city of around 50,000 people and the county seat of Hall County. The town is still called The City of Grand Island, despite the fact the channels have shifted and the island no longer exists.

No ancient stone monoliths to bring to mind the mysterious stone circles of British Isles? Well, you are in luck. Just outside Alliance, Nebraska, on the edge of the Sandhills (which themselves are just grass-covered sand dunes), rise thirty-eight vintage American automobiles arranged in a precise recreation of Stonehenge. The art installation is known as Carhenge. The designer and artist, Jim Reinders, conceived of it as a memorial to his late father. Grampa, with his own fondness for American-made vehicles, insisted we stop for pictures.

When we visited, Carhenge felt so quintessentially American. A gesture that captured the boundless, absurd, and at times reckless creativity of our country better than nearly anything I'd ever come across. Perhaps that was why Grampa and Leo could see past its *kitsch* and felt only fondness for it.

Photo: *Neill in front of Carhenge in Alliance, Nebraska.*

But back to Leo and Ogallala, where Leo hosted us. The town was also home to "Front Street," a faux western town that is one of the main tourist draws. On Front Street I could not escape Grampa handing me my Stetson, which I had "forgotten" in the car, as he took pictures of me outside of Cowboy's Rest Saloon.

With Leo, we continued northwest along Highway 26 and the North Platte River, stopping along the way at Ash Hallow State Park, near the town of Blue Creek. There I climbed up Windlass Hill. Ash Hallow was a gateway to the North Platte Valley for wagon trains throughout the late 1800s. Windlass Hill is still scarred with ruts from their wheels.

Photo: View from the top of Windlass Hill in Ash Hallow State Park.

      We passed through Oshkosh, Broadwater, and Bridgeport, Nebraska, towards the national monuments of Chimney Rock and Scotts Bluff. As I read historical markers explaining the spiritual significance of the landmarks to the original tribes of the region, [10] playing cowboy with the Stetson felt even less appropriate. My reluctance was lost on Grampa and Leo but visible in the pictures Grampa took. My angst abated, however, when we learned what the Lakota Sioux, displaced to the plains from the Great Lakes region, had called Chimney Rock. Through a quirk of cosmic symmetry, the tribe's name for the phallic-shaped Arikaree sandstone translated directly as "Elk Penis."

---

[10] Arapaho, Arikara, Cheyenne, Crow, Hidatsas, Kiowas, Mandans, Pawnee, Poncas, and Shoshone, among others.

Photos: Views of Chimney Rock.

After Chimney Rock, we drove on to Scotts Bluff. I wanted to stretch my legs, and so I ran all the way up the trail to the top of the cliffs. Leo and Grampa waited in the car, reminiscing. The five bluffs of Scotts Bluff National Monument are some of the highest points in Nebraska. The pass through them was the last major milestone before wagon trains would begin an increasingly steep climb into the Rockies.

Photo: Views from the top of Scotts Bluff, and standing outside the historical barracks at Fort Robinson.

I look back at the afternoon now, remembering how I had tried to see the landscape first from the perspective of indigenous peoples and then the white Europeans who pushed them out. I was unsure whether to respect the courage of the intrepid American pioneers or decry the land theft and genocide they took part in. But today, after reading Grampa's memoir, I try to suspend analysis and simply consider how the country, the state would have looked to two young men of sixteen in the late 1930s.

In the midst of the great depression, when Grampa and Leo were trying to find careers, trying to imagine how they would make their own marks on the world, grown men wandered the streets looking for work, bank runs were common, and families filled up breadlines, the faces of mothers and children leaned out from starvation, their clothes threadbare. On the horizon, apocalyptic sandstorms blackened the sky and swept streams of dust into streets already blasted by a summer sun—a sun that offered no relief from the long, disastrous droughts of the 1930s.

I realize that, in this setting, thirty dollars for fifteen days of work would have seemed a fortune to two teenage boys, having grown up working on the family farm for nothing. The possibilities and horrors of what Grampa and Leo would face in Europe were just that: possibilities—distant ones at that. They figured the greatest discomforts they might face in the Nebraska National Guard would be trainings stateside. An uncomfortable night sleeping on the ground here, a long march there. Not much more strenuous than working sunup to sundown on the farm. These were small prices to pay for the certainty of knowing where your next shirt, your next pair of boots, your next meal would come from, especially when farms were being foreclosed upon and the banks doing the foreclosing were becoming insolvent.

The army Grampa described in his memoir is nothing like the digitized, laser-guided marvel we have today. But even that is indicative of the privation of the failed farms and job shortages he and Leo were fleeing. Grampa writes of riding on train carriages from the 1800s—not even World War I vintage but with the feel and look of the Civil War. During winter trainings, he and Leo huddled together at night more like refugees themselves than liberators. The post-war years of affluence were non-existent for the teenage versions of Grampa and Leo. When they were young, large pockets of states were still wilderness. The "great powers" were still all in Europe, and *their* power was growing, under democracies *and* authoritarian regimes. They had the edge in technology and military might. Headlines from the era spread the alarm of gas attacks and of U-boats menacing the shores. Most of the sentinel towers erected on the east and west coasts of the US are long since gone, but not all of them. Some remain, concrete relics that most of us take for old lighthouses. With crops failing, rivers drying up, and those black-brown walls of dust looming over midwestern towns, the American experiment must have seemed as precarious then as it feels now.

Joining the National Guard, even if Grampa and Leo had to lie about their ages to do so, gave them an escape. Even more so, it gave the pride and purpose that young men have searched for from time immemorial. Edward Tick, in his book *War and the Soul,* describes how military training orients the initiate to their place in the world . . . their role in society. Enlisting would have been attractive to me had I been in Grampa and Leo's shoes. The government offered the only way out of a region that was increasingly coming to resemble a blighted hellscape.

The irony, of course, was that Grampa and Leo would march from one hell to another. But they couldn't have foreseen that then. When they enlisted, they saw the promise of a paycheck—*at least.* At best, they saw a vocation that was akin to the archetypal quest, the hero's journey. Tick reminds us that this rite of passage is universal in human society. It is an opportunity for young people to endure an ordeal, *the* ordeal, that will forever define them. It's the quest story, from Jason and the Argonauts, to Theseus and the Minotaur, to the likes of Bilbo Baggins or Luke Skywalker. The quest narrative is characterized by reoccurring guides. Their forms are familiar to us: oracles, hoary wizards, Jedi masters, or even drill sergeants. The quest transforms the youth into an adult, the boy into a man. Thus tested, they return with status and respect, whether as prince, ringbearer, Jedi master, or decorated military officer. Then, the adult can take their place in society with honor and provide for him or herself, their family, and the next generation.

All along the way, Grampa and Leo would have been reminded of this. As they passed from one milestone to the next, the signs of symbols of military service shored up their identity, validating their choices. Just as the sign over the barracks at Fort Robinson did, as it read: "Through these Portals Pass the Army's Best Horsemen." Even though he had not been a member of the mounted cavalry, when we visited Camp Robinson, Grampa insisted I stand under that sign so he could take a picture. It was a nod to tradition that was more important than the distinction between cavalry versus infantry.

For Grampa and Leo, they all were the Army's greatest; this orientation would last a lifetime.

After our afternoon at Scotts Bluff, we drove back to Ogallala. We ate supper at a diner where Leo knew all the waitresses by name. When we were finished, Leo took us on a driving tour of his neighborhood—which after six or seven blocks ran all out of houses and other buildings. Soon there was nothing but farmland to the left and right of the car. Still, we kept driving, down the plain, unswerving roads that mark the grid lines between cornfields. A cloud of dust, lit golden by the setting sun, rose in our wake. Leo pointed out pheasants, which he said he would have shot with the shotgun he kept in the trunk—had they been in season.

Long after the houses of Ogallala had disappeared over the horizon, as the sun was streaming into our eyes, Leo pointed with his chin to something off to the side of the road. His skin, pale from long days spent indoors, took on a ruddy glow in the orange light. For a moment he looked hearty and rugged. His eyes, glaucous and filmed with cataracts, narrowed in a defiant squint. He was reminiscent of a sea captain standing on the prow of his ship. Grampa shaded his own eyes, his hand in a salute, a blade over his brow.

Leo pulled us off the main road into a nondescript patch of fallow field, distinguished only by the rectangle of chain-link fence topped with razor wire in its center. The gate in the fence held a rusted sign reading, "US Government Property. No Trespassing." It felt abandoned, with creepers twined in the fence and a pile of hotdog wrappers and faded 7-11 Big Gulp cups piled at the base.

Despite the dilapidated air of the place, I read solemnity and familiarity in both men. I had seen it before in Grampa, when he had taken me to the Army base back in Omaha for dinners in the officer's club, where young guards in uniform snapped to attention to salute him and Coco as they rolled up to the traffic gate, two seniors in a Lincoln Town Car, who might normally go unnoticed anywhere else.

Leo explained that this spot was an underground missile silo. It was where the North American Aerospace Defense Command (NORAD as he still called it) kept some of its nuclear-tipped ICBMs, standing at the ready, even in 1995, to fire off in the direction of the former Soviet Union. The silo was not much to look at. The facility was completely below ground, the grass on the other side of the gate overgrown. There was nothing to see but the fence, silhouetted against a sky that had turned to the color of butterscotch. Crickets were chirping and meadowlarks flitted over the fence, undeterred by the security measures. A wall of unharvested corn lined the farthest perimeter, the tasseled heads waving in the breeze. The tranquility belied the world-ending technology waiting just beneath the concrete cap—if indeed this silo wasn't decommissioned, which I suspected it was. One could almost forget it had ever posed any threat whatsoever.

But Leo hadn't, nor Grampa. For them, the righteous fight, their opposition against Evil Empires, still gave them their sense of purpose, a sanctity to their identities, an antagonist for their narratives, and a destination for their quest. And after all, their loyalty had been rewarded with status, honor, self-respect—not to mention paychecks, benefits, and the pensions they both lived on in retirement.

They had returned with treasure after all.

So of course, Leo's "neighborhood" included the members of missile command who lived and slept through their shifts, deep below the earth, ready to strike back at an enemy that *might* still threaten the US. Who knew for sure? The Russians were wily, or so Leo said. These missile command crews—real or no—were more than neighbors; they were Grampa and Leo's brethren. In their continued vigilance, they saw their own.

The two old men still lived their lives in reference to the system that they had served and that had served them, even the possibly abandoned nodes of it. I think they took comfort in proximity to the symbols of war that endured even in peacetime, the outposts of the military they had left behind, "stronger than ever." It all spoke to a dependable meritocracy and moral clarity. One that feels so absent today.

But in 1995, it still gave two old vets their place in the world.

RECOLLECTIONS OF A GI
II.
Robert Lewis Fowler

Mobilization: December, 1940

Sometime in early December, 1940 we received word that we would be officially mobilized on December 23rd. We were told to notify our employers, if we were lucky enough to be employed. I was working for Beuchene & Wolber, an automotive body and paint shop, making ten or twelve bucks a week. I would make less as a corporal in the army, except I would get room and board plus clothing (uniforms).

We all reported to the Armory on the 23rd and were sworn in. They started giving physicals. I was greatly shocked when I found out I failed my physical. They heard a rattle in my lungs. I had to talk real fast to Captain Kelso. He finally agreed to sign a waiver for me. I actually had paint dust in my lungs from work. It cleared up as soon as I got away from the paint and into plenty of outside fresh air, which wasn't hard to find once in the Army.

My next problem was on the 5th or 6th of January, 1940. I came down with the flu and was sent to Fort Crook to the Post Hospital the very day the outfit pulled out for Camp Robinson, Arkansas. I did recover quickly and was transferred to the 17th Infantry on Post for rations and quarters while I was waiting for orders to be mailed back from Camp Robinson. (While in the hospital I learned that diarrhea and bed pans and loss of balance can produce a serious crisis. I have never used one since.)

Arkansas: Camp Robinson, January-June, 1941

It was close to the end of January 1941 before I finally received travel orders to proceed to Camp Robinson. During my stay with the 17th Infantry, I was introduced to the new Garand M1 rifle and had a little experience with it before it was ever issued to the 134th. The 35th Division was still wearing WWI helmets, breeches, and fatigue clothes. We were told we had to wear them out before replacement. There were numerous "accidents" and tears. Some people took turns dragging their buddies on the seat of their pants till they were worn through. If you were the "dragee" it wasn't difficult to tell when that point was reached. We non-commissioned officers (NCOs) were allowed to wear slacks with our uniform blouse if we bought them ourselves.

1941 was famous (or infamous) for lack of weapons and equipment. We did complete all our training, including Louisiana maneuvers, but it was a struggle.

January 1941 was spent setting up the camp area and in a few classes on military courtesy and some of the basics. On the first of February that same year, the Army was allowed to go to wartime strength. Rifle companies were allowed to go to 217 men. Of the many lucky ones such as myself, there was a promotion for almost every one of the original ninety-six members of our company. I wound up as one of the twenty-four three-stripe sergeants. Soon recruits started coming in; all of them were from Nebraska through the Selective Service program. Everyone was in for one year, which was the original term specified by the draft. Most of our new people had volunteered through the draft system so as to get their year over quickly. A big percentage of the new people were from farms or small towns. They made superb soldiers and later became NCOs themselves. Many of these people became some of my best and closest friends. I still visit and share many memories with those that made it back home.

March 1941, we were issued the new Garand M1 Rifle. We had them just long enough to learn how to use them. They were withdrawn and issued to "someone who needed them worse than we did." Then, instead of getting our 03 Springfields back, we were issued the old British Enfield. WHAT A BLOW! The cocking stroke was opposite the Springfield, and it threw us off our timing in rapid fire on the range. The next issue was the Sun-Tan uniforms along with the snafu hat, the ugliest and most worthless headgear ever issued by Uncle Sam. We lost our campaign hats, the Smokey hats worn today by a lot of Highway Patrol Officers and used by many drill instructors in the Army and Marines. We felt the loss. One welcome item issued were the canvas leggings or "putts." They didn't even bother asking us to turn in our wrap leggings. They took their place in infamy with the snafu hat. Eventually the blue fatigues were worn out and replaced by ODs and a better design also. This became our day-to-day drill uniform. We still had the WWI flat steel helmets and kept them until sometime the following year. By the middle of 1941, wool slacks were a permanent part of our "A" uniform, and the breeches were "I-and-I-ed"—a term for turning in for scrap.

In order to fulfill the training mission after new selectees joined us, the NCOs that were considered qualified instructors were divided into two groups. One group worked with the "old" men, and the other group was assigned to a training battalion. Joe Jelinek and I were assigned as acting first sergeants and instructors to give basic training to the new men, who had been organized into temporary squads, platoons, and companies. At different times I had First Lt. Boatsman and Second Lt. Fran Mason as acting commanders. Boatsman went on to become regimental commander in combat. Mason became a company commander with an outstanding combat reputation.

We were involved in this training activity for about two months. It was beneficial to most of us, certainly to me. As noted before, I was commanding men even fifteen years older than myself. We had to study every night to be prepared for the subjects scheduled for the next day. I became twenty years old on the 24th of April, 1941. On my record I was twenty-two. I had not found it necessary yet to shave every day. I started smoking cigars (BIG ones) and chewing tobacco in order to appear older. Years later, I found out the men had nicknamed me "Cupie," short for "Cupid." I sure am glad I didn't know it at the time.

Photo: Fowler at camp—year unknown—smoking to look older.

After basic training was completed, everyone returned to their parent companies for Phase Two, which was basic unit training.

Captain Kelso took me aside one day and explained how the new Table of Organization (TOE) would work. Each platoon had four squads with a three stripe or "buck" sergeant, squad leader, assistant squad leader, and corporal. There was also a buck sergeant platoon guide and a buck platoon sergeant. Due to my "seniority," and despite my real age, I was considered one of the senior buck sergeants and would be the next platoon sergeant if a vacancy occurred. Captain Kelso had a need for someone with a halfway decent IQ to fill the communication and reconnaissance sergeant position. He pointed out that, because of the technical knowledge required and responsibility of the job, it would certainly be upgraded before any of the other posts. If I took the job I also knew my buddy, Leo Samson, would get my old job. In view of all this, I accepted the assignment. The job required a thorough knowledge of the operation and maintenance of the "walkie talkie" radios and the telephones. I would have to become an expert map reader and pathfinder scout for the company commander. I was excited by the challenge.

I would have four company runners that I would have to teach what I would learn at the Regimental School. It developed that I had to do all the map reading instruction for the whole company because the only other people that knew that subject were officers and they were in short supply. We were supposed to have six, and we seldom had more than two. In addition to my other duties, I was also the platoon sergeant in charge of company headquarters. This consisted of mess sergeant, supply sergeant, eight cooks and assistant cooks, artificer, company clerk, two truck drivers, and a motor corporal. At parade-type formations I had to try to make these specialists types look like soldiers. So I was considered a platoon sergeant, even though at times I had only my runners under my direct control.

Later I found that my most important jobs were (1) knowing where we were on the map at all times, (2) knowing where our headquarters was located, and (3) knowing the locations of the headquarters of our neighboring companies. I accompanied the company commander in the field almost all the time and took notes at important meetings. This did give me a chance to meet people from other units and to know who the other officers in the regiment were and what the assignments were.

At this time in 1941, the 35th Division was a "square division" made up of two brigades, the 69th and 70th. Each brigade had two regiments. The 69th had the 134th from Nebraska and the 137th from Kansas. The 70th had two regiments from Missouri, the 138th and 140th. Each regiment had three battalions (Rifle) and a support battalion. Each battalion had three rifle companies and a support company. I was in the Third Battalion of the 134th Infantry Regiment, Company L. The Third Battalion consisted of I, K, and L Rifle Companies and M Company, which was support with heavy machine guns and 80 MM mortars. The rifle companies had three rifle platoons and a support platoon, which had two light machine gun sections and two 60 MM mortar squads making the mortar section. Each unit also had a headquarters. Squads had their squad leader (second lieutenants) and two runners. Companies had a commanding officer, an executive officer, a first sergeant, a company clerk, and myself, along with all the people listed earlier. Battalions and all the larger units had headquarters, commanding officers, as well as other support type units. There was the Medical Company, the Service Company, the Anti-tank Company, and the Howitzer or Cannon Company. Medical Company was trained and supplied by the 110th Medical Regiment. Service Company provided chow and all other supplies such as clothing, water, and ammunition. Also, there was a clerical section for record keeping and general clerical activities in a regiment of 3,500 men.

Also, there was a large transportation section with many 2-1/2-ton trucks and various other vehicles.

Anti-tank Company was just that. They had 37 MM guns and the necessary transportation to employ them wherever needed. Biggest problem was the German-made tanks, which were too tough to be hurt by a little 37 MM shell.

Howitzer Company later became Cannon Company and was really a battery of 105 MM artillery.

Regimental Headquarters Command had clerks, lots of common equipment, an intelligence and reconnaissance platoon, and a pioneer platoon which could construct small bridges or build road blocks.

After individual basic and unit basic training came advanced individual and unit training. Units of all sizes started learning how to work as a team and to depend on each other for their assigned missions. Unit pride and *"esprit de corps"* was starting to develop. The regimental band, which at that time was attached to Service Company for rations and quarters, consisted of about thirty-five men. They were very good at playing "There Is No Place like Nebraska" at 0600 every morning except Sunday while they marched around the regimental area. This was also our marching song at numerous parades and reviews.

We started thinking we were the best company in the best regiment in the best division in the United States Army!!

In June 1941, Captain Kelso was transferred to Company A as commanding officer and Captain Ray Thurman of A Company was made CO of Company L. He was a kindly small man, very friendly and easy to get along with. He made very few changes in the unit, and the men of L Company accepted him very quickly. Captain Thurman was very patient and taught me many things about my job in the field.

Photo: Telegram from Evelyn with a clipping from the Omaha World Herald showing Fowler with his first daughter, Kathleen, while on leave from training, post-war, 1948).

Louisiana: August, 1941

We went to the Louisiana maneuvers in August and spent a couple months "playing war." It seemed most of our time was spent doing long marches at night. The first one was 25 miles and it was pretty tough on some of the guys. I had one man in my section who was a big tall farm boy type, and he used to razz me about being a kid. After we got to our destination I challenged him to a wrestling match. It was then I had fun. Even though I was only 140 pounds and 5'9" and pretty slim, I was in good shape and could tough it out fairly well.

We spent most of our time in Louisiana. Always we bivouacked in timber and swamp areas so as to be unseen by enemy aircraft. But a different kind of enemy had scouted our position: the biting and blood-sucking kind. But even with rattlers, copperheads, and mosquitos, we suffered surprisingly small numbers of casualties due to advances in antivenom and other medicine. I tasted rattle snake meat for the first time. Real good! It reminded me of shrimp.

More long marches! I remember one of about 32 miles. It started around noon and was supposed to be a strategic withdrawal (fancy term for retreat). We walked most of the day and well into the night. About midnight, after covering more than 25 miles, there were a few trucks available for the people with bad feet, etc. I was helping one of my men into a truck and here came my brother Jim. I knew that his feet were bleeding, but I asked him, "Where you going, Junior?" He called me a few "unprintables" and went back to formation and finished out the march.

I was called to battalion headquarters a few times to help in map reading and recon missions, which boosted my ego quite a bit. Captain Thurman had been assigned as temporary battalion executive officer and First Lt. Moose Larson was acting commander for L Company. Larson was a rather big guy, and once in a while he would get bent out of shape for some reason and would take off through the woods, looking for someone to chew out. The warning cry that echoed through the timber was "The Moose is on the loose!"

Arkansas: Camp Robinson, October, 1941

In early October the mock battle was over, and we were returned to dear old Camp Robinson, just a few miles north of Little Rock. One incident on the way home caused a nickname for the 35th Division.

Due to a lack of trucks to carry all the Division at once, we were shuttled—riding a while and walking a while. One unit was going past a country club golf course while a group of people were playing. A couple of shapely ladies in shorts were part of the golf group. Naturally there were a few yelps and whistles. As it happened, one of the golfers was Lieutenant General Ben Lear, who took great offense. That unit of GIs was immediately trucked back down the line and then had 15 miles to walk again and think about their sins. Newspapers learned of the incident, and quite a bit of publicity ensued. From then on, the 35th was the "YOO HOO DIVISION".

In spite of all this, the Division was welcomed back to Arkansas and Little Rock as conquering heroes, with the city-wide celebrations of parades, street dances, and carnivals. We weren't sure what we had done to deserve all this, but it didn't take long to find out.

A couple days after the 35th left Camp Robinson for maneuvers, the Sixth Division moved into the camp as a stop-over *en route* to maneuvers. They were allowed to go into Little Rock on pass, and they proceeded to get a little rowdy. In addition, most of them had a Brooklyn accent. These "Damn Yankees" never had a chance to endear themselves to the citizens of Arkansas. It got so bad the town was declared "off limits" for the whole outfit. The 35th Division consisted of men from Missouri, Kansas, and Nebraska, with the majority of them being from farms and small towns. They were considered gentlemen, and many of the men married Little Rock girls. The Governor of Arkansas had already declared the 35th Division the Adopted Sons of Arkansas.

After we were back and settled into our routine training, furloughs were allowed, fifty percent of the unit at a time. This was my chance to become a car owner. I bought a 1939 Plymouth and rented it to six guys for ten dollars each to take on furlough back to Nebraska. I took it and five guys when it came my turn on furlough. This helped me pay off the car. I also ran a taxi service into Little Rock on Saturdays.

Photo: Fowler had a lifelong love affair with automobiles, and buying his first one was a proud moment for him.

Armistice Day, 1941, was a special event. The 134th was asked to parade in Memphis, Tennessee. We made special preparations, our wool class As were freshly cleaned and pressed. All canvas and cartridge belts were scrubbed with GI soap, and the best pair of GI shoes was polished to perfection. Helmets were freshly painted, and all equipment and clothing went into our extra footlocker, which was not touched until just before parade time. All this effort produced as fine a looking regiment as ever was assembled. After the parade, the local newspapers paid lavish compliments to the 134th. The other military units that participated didn't even come close in appearance. That evening, after the parade, we were turned loose on pass and there was a dance at the city auditorium. There were plenty of southern lasses to go around. No one lacked a dancing partner.

REFLECTIONS V.
Promiscuity
Ted Neill

It is strange to read the sections describing dance halls and dance partners in 1941 and not cast a skeptical eye. Grampa had been married in March of that very year. It was even stranger to read Grampa's memoirs and see Grandma Evelyn go completely unmentioned.

There were reasons for this. All of them somewhat uncomfortable. One was the knowledge we all carried with us that, after the war, with my mother still young but old enough to remember a pervasive sadness around the house, Grampa had "stepped out" on Evelyn. Not only that, he had gotten this mystery mistress pregnant. This "other woman" ended up having a miscarriage, but Grampa, according to stories passed down to me in hushed side-conversations with my aunts, had been ready to leave Evelyn for this woman. Indeed, they were certain Grampa would have and was planning it, but she had broken off the relationship.

I can only imagine this contributed to the emotional turbulence and reckless drinking that would rock the family in subsequent years.

Photo Next Page: Robert and Evelyn on their wedding day, March 15th, 1941.

There is something poignant to me in the fact that in the only pictures I have of Robert and Evelyn from their wedding day are pictures in which they are standing separate from one another. Those pictures were taken on a military base the day of their ceremony. I don't know if it is from the sun in their eyes or something else, but I read a certain fatalism in their expressions in place of the joy I am used to seeing in other newlywed pictures. By all accounts, and my own experience, Grampa and Grandma had a fulfilling marriage, but this was only later in life, not in the beginning or during the years my aunts and uncles were children. Knowing what was ahead of them, it's hard to look at those pictures of Bob and Evelyn and not feel a sense of foreboding.

The other complication related to Evelyn's absence from Grampa's narrative is the fact that it was Coco who was typing up the first half of it. I imagine it would have been a bit awkward, even after Evelyn's death, for Grampa to wax on at length about his first wife to his second, especially with the whispered rumors in the family that Coco was actually the very woman Grampa had stepped out with decades before.

Whether or not Coco was indeed the "other woman," as Grampa's infidelity came to light among his children and grandchildren, it was a black mark against him for all of us. And it's hard for me to read those passages about dance halls, which I am certain have been sanitized in his retelling, and not wonder what betrayals might have occurred that we will never hear about.

His infidelities were an aspect of Grampa's shadow self that, along with his drinking, left so many scars, unanswered questions, and resentments amid two generations of family and friends. His cheating was especially shocking to his grandchildren, who had only known him as the one-dimensional, avuncular war hero: Grampa.

Edward Tick helped me, in some fashion, to understand this. Not to exonerate or excuse Grampa's choices, but, like his drinking, a part of me does recognize the further signs of trauma, at least in his post-war infidelity. Sexual promiscuity, along with drug/alcohol use and other high-risk behaviors, is common among veterans. These behaviors re-create the adrenaline-fueled high of combat, mitigate the depression/anxiety that plagues so many soldiers afterwards, or both. For men whose moral compasses were rocked by the experience of taking lives, young men whose souls were fractured by combat and loss, vets who did not receive the requisite counseling or ritual reentry into civilian society that was needed for their return for healing and reintegration into society, affairs were commonplace, just like nightmares, flashbacks, and even high rates of domestic violence.

In the 1940s and 1950s, there wasn't even much vocabulary to talk about post-traumatic stress. I remember Grampa telling me that it was *years* after the war that he and his buddies even disclosed to one another that they still had nightmares. My mother and her contemporaries would talk about how, even into the 1950s, there was still a sense of post-war euphoria. Yet, on the periphery of the anniversary parades and Remembrance Day marches, there were always the disheveled men hovering in the shadows, alleyways, and under bridges. These veterans were homeless, drunk, and wrecked, no longer able to participate in society, much less a day of celebration. These were the men who died of exposure, alcohol poisoning, drug overdoses, or suicide, even while their brothers in arms kept up appearances, held down jobs, raised families, but wrestled with demons—demons that often only the women sleeping next to them during their night terrors knew about. And these were women who were shamed and humiliated by betrayals but, because of the mores of the time, kept silent and remained with their men. Some of them, like Evelyn, turned to drink to help drown out her own feelings of hurt, resentment, and betrayal.

Half or so of my thirteen cousins struggle with substance abuse. I never have, even when I suffered debilitating depression and anxiety. But I do remember my own revolving carousel of dead end relationships—my own version of Grampa's promiscuity—as I rode the carousel from one relationship to another in my twenties and early thirties. I was compelled by the notion that in the next relationship, the next passionate rendezvous, I might find some sense of thrill, some healing, or some purpose, all of which were lacking as I careened about the world, my own sense of morality shattered by the experience of watching so many children die in my arms. And in the powerlessness one feels after witnessing the death and suffering of others, the romantic tryst, even the accumulation of them, becomes a compensation of a sort. Like any other kind of misuse and abuse, it only leaves one empty. Perhaps the worst aspect of gratifying your spiritual emptiness through romantic trysts, is that it abuses, debases, and objectifies the partner. If there are vows broken or children left, the hurts run even deeper, crossing over to the next generation.

     Despite what we who are guilty of this might tell ourselves, it's never a victimless transgression, never a harmless indiscretion, and never without meaning. Such betrayals, the objectification, the *mis*-using, and the discarding of partners in such a selfish way, follows us to our graves and even beyond.

RECOLLECTIONS OF A GI
III.
Robert Lewis Fowler

Moving West: December, 1941

Pearl Harbor

The next event of importance was the one that changed everyone's lives. It happened on a Sunday when I was the acting first sergeant. As was the practice, the senior sergeants had to fill in on weekends, even though there normally was no training. One of us had to be present, just in case. Everything was normal around the company area until the news over the radio announced that Pearl Harbor had been bombed by the Japanese. I think we all aged a couple years in a very few minutes.

Brother Jim, Tom Ryan, and Jack Blunk had borrowed the car that weekend, and they were a little late in getting back to camp. The wild stories of the attack and people's reaction to the news were next to unbelievable. The order had been put out over the radio for all troops to report back to camp as soon as possible.

The next week was filled with preparation for movement, which we were expecting although the actual order had not been issued. Most of us had two footlockers. There was one which we had used prior to mobilization and one that was regular issue after we arrived at Robinson in January that year. Our personal locker was to be sent home with all our belongings that were not GI.

During this time there were some people whose enlistments had run out. Normally this would mean they would be honorably discharged unless they chose to re-up. Some of them made it as far as the pay window at the finance office. However, the order came out that everyone was "in" for the duration of the war. When time or the future was mentioned from then on, everything was "for the duration." But there was never any doubt that someday the war would end and that we would be victorious.

After maneuvers in late 1941, the draft law concerning maximum age was changed. About fifteen or twenty people were sent home because they were too old. Original max age was thirty-five. Now it was twenty-eight. However, all these people were called up later and returned to their units.

On December 14, 1941, one week after the attack on Pearl Harbor, we received orders to move by rail. Destination unknown. Following a week of preparation, this was accomplished very easily. After boarding the train and settling down to looking out the windows and speculating on our classified destination, we at least figured out we were heading west. To us, this meant we were bound for the South Pacific. We had been training for almost a year and had been through all phases, so we expected to go overseas immediately.

Denver, Colorado

Our first stopover was Denver. We were allowed to get off the train and exercise. But the layover didn't last long. We left Denver and started the climb up the mountains. This was a real treat for most of us, who had never seen the mountains except in pictures. We had to lower the shades on the train at dark, but at one point, I peeked out and saw beautiful moonlight on fresh snow. I learned later that it was Donner Pass. The sightseeing was wonderful, but the rest of the trip was miserable—old, antiquated coaches, three men *and* equipment per two seats. We found out the hard way that going through tunnels with the windows open was not very smart. The coal-fired steam engines made quite a bit of soot and smoke. Five days of this made that first shower very, very welcome.

California: 1942

Fort Ord

We finally found out that our destination was Fort Ord, California, when we arrived there.

Fort Ord looked real nice. There were barracks instead of five-men tents, and the California weather was welcome. We had a few days to spend getting settled in before Christmas. On Christmas Eve we received orders to fall out with full field pack, which included a shelter half and two blankets. We were moved out to the hills and set up a field bivouac. The reason was that they wanted us out of the area over the holidays because of the possibility of the Japanese bombing us. Pearl Harbor had occurred on Sunday, and if it were going to happen to the West Coast, the holidays were the expected time. The same procedure was carried out over New Year's.

San Luis Obispo

We were scheduled to ship out from Fort Ord to San Francisco and then board ships there. I learned later that this did not happen because of a vessel shortage. We did leave Fort Ord in

January 1942 and wound up in Camp San Luis Obispo, which was south of Fort Ord, about halfway to Los Angeles. We had a mountain close by our company area, and we flat-landers got our exercise climbing it. We had beach landing training in this area for about two months and then were assigned to the Southern California Defense Command. Our first assignment was El Cerrito, California, a small community just north of Berkeley. We were up near the top of a high hill using a Boy Scout camp as our billets. There were several small cabins in and around an old quarry. Our mission was to operate roving patrols between defense plants, hopefully to prevent sabotage. My job was to reconnoiter each plant and its surrounding area, decide on the best emergency approach, and lay out several alternate routes for routine patrolling. We were to vary our routes and timing so that there was never anything done repetitively on any recognizable schedule.

We were provided with several GI staff cars and several three-quarter ton trucks. Each vehicle carried a team of four men, one of whom was an NCO in charge. Our area consisted mostly of ship-building plants, including the Kaiser Company, which became famous for making Liberty Ships. There were thousands of these ships made for the Merchant Marines. Many were sunk in later battles, but Kaiser could build them faster than the enemy could sink them.

Catalina Island

We had this duty for two or three months. Then we were assembled as a regiment in an area south of San Francisco. We found out later that we could expect to be rotated with other units every three months for all the time we were assigned to this duty.

Then the whole regiment was sent to the Inglewood racetrack. After spending a few hours cleaning the horse stalls to make living quarters, we were ordered to fall in with all our equipment. We boarded trucks and wound up at Fort MacArthur and marched over to a pier in San Pedro harbor.

We had received a new company commander, Captain Paul H. Jacobs, before leaving Camp Robinson. He had a sense of humor and took pleasure in keeping our destination secret as we boarded water taxis and proceeded across the San Pedro Channel to Catalina Island. Very few of us had ever seen this much water, and the flying fish were really a strange sight.

We were billeted in a cabin camp, and everyone had a good place to live. I was sent out to the mission sites the first thing and later returned to guide our men up into position. Sometime around the first of the year, a Japanese submarine had surfaced near Santa Barbara and shelled some oil tanks on shore. This had people concerned that the Japanese might attempt an invasion of the West Coast. As a consequence, two radar positions were set up on Catalina Island, which is 26 miles out from Los Angeles. Our mission was to provide infantry protection for the radar sets and their crews. There were outposts placed all along the West Coast, and the 35th Division was spread over most of the lower half of the state. This also included men patrolling the beaches. Our company was organized into two tactical groups. One group would spend a week up at the site areas, while the other would remain in Avalon and train. The training schedule was very relaxed, and while in Avalon the men had time to enjoy the facilities that many tourists had spent a lot of money to see.

Catalina was owned by the Wrigley family—the chewing gum company. There were approximately 1,000 people living on the island year-round, and they were allowed to remain even during this time. Also, we were allowed to have wives and close family join us. It was a good example of the old expression: "We never had it so good."

Ventura

But every good thing has to come to an end, and after three months we were sent back to the mainland and located at the Municipal Airport near the North American Aircraft factory. We had ground security, as well as motorized emergency teams on half-track and light tanks. We escorted aircraft convoys to the piers and for shipment overseas. Three months later we were sent to Ventura and assigned to beach patrol and outposts along the shore. I was temporarily assigned to Third Battalion Intelligence Section. There were outposts along the cliffs near the shore. They were a couple of miles apart, but each one could see some of the area of the outposts on either side. No vessel was allowed closer than one mile off shore in the daytime and three miles at night. Any two of the outposts could take a compass reading on a vessel and phone this to me. Knowing the outpost locations, I could triangulate the intersection of the two readings placed on a map and pinpoint the exact location. If they were too close, I would call the Coast Guard and they would take it from there. After three months in Ventura we were assembled up at Ojai Country Club. Temporary barracks had been built on part of the golf course.

During the time we were in California the 35th Division was organized into the triangular concept. The best description was three smaller units made up the next larger unit. The 138th and 140th regiments were taken from the division and reassigned. Also, the Second Battalion of the 134th was sent to the Aleutian Islands. A new regiment was assigned to the 35th Division. The 320th Infantry was activated, and NCOs and some officers were transferred to the 320th, plus the Second Battalion of the 134th was replaced with NCOs and officers from the First and Third Battalions, and replacements were assigned to us from Camp Roberts. This meant that all three battalions had many new men who had basic training only. We were sent back to San Luis Obispo, and it was there that we received the replacements and reorganized.

REFLECTIONS VI.
Evelyn & Elyse
Ted Neill

When Evelyn was dying from cancer in 1991, my mother went to Omaha for a few weeks to be with her. Mom stayed with my Grampa, making daily visits to Evelyn in the hospital. Grandma Evelyn was in and out of consciousness, frequently coming to and asking if my mother was still there in the room with her. Together they watched the San Francisco 49ers, since Evelyn professed an outspoken and unabashed love for Joe Montana. She had a full-length, signed poster of Joe in her room back home that her daughters had given her for her birthday. The poster was one of Evelyn's most treasured possessions.

We never told her that my aunt Elyse had forged the signature.

But after Mom's penultimate visit with her mother, driving home, the knowledge that the next time she would see her mother would be the last crushed her. She drove back to her parents' place fighting for composure, tears blurring her vision. When she finally parked in the driveway she rushed into the house, a grown woman only in appearance. Inside she was a little girl, about to lose her mother and seeking the comfort of her father.

Instead she found Bob sitting in the kitchen, drinking for the first time in almost twenty-five years, the bottle nearly empty beside him. He was too drunk to feel a sense of shame to hide it.

"All I wanted was my father in that moment," Mom told me years later, reflecting on the disappointment of that afternoon.

It would only be a slip, not a full-blown relapse, but timing was everything. When Mom needed Grampa, drink had taken him away.

Again.

Mom left the house without a word, walked all the way to her sister Mary Anne's home, crashed down on the couch, and cried there for the next couple hours.

It was vintage Robert Lewis Fowler, a sad, stinging reminder to my mother that he had never really changed, a rebuke to her and all her sisters for ever hoping otherwise.

But their hope was not baseless. Grampa's valor, his courage on the battlefield, stood in stark contrast to his shortcomings as a father. When the stakes had been life or death, Grampa had stood in the gap. His medals, his wounds, the bullet he still carried in his hip until the day he died, testified to that truth.

And it was not as if my aunts and uncles had been without examples from childhood of Grampa coming through as a father. One story my aunt Elyse still recalls is how one morning while cooking breakfast—Elyse was always in the kitchen; even as a child she loved to cook—she spilled grease on her nightgown, and it caught fire. Elyse, not knowing better, rushed to the sink where one of her siblings slapped the faucet lever to run cold water and douse the fire.

Grampa knew the only way to put out a grease fire was to smother it. Water would only make things worse. He kicked his chair out from behind him, raced across the kitchen, and grabbed Elyse up in his arms before she reached the sink. Without regard for himself, he hugged his panicked daughter against his own chest to put out the fire.

Elyse escaped the ordeal with only a small burn near her collar bone. She remembers that moment with clarity, even all these years later. Not because of the danger or the fear of flames. She remembers it because it was the only time her father ever hugged her.

As I contemplate my mother weeping on the couch that afternoon, knowing her mother was about to die, having been let down by her father *yet again,* it feels like such a sad tragedy to reflect that the one time Robert Fowler embraced his third-born child, Elyse, it left a scar that would last a lifetime.

RECOLLECTIONS OF A GI
IV.
Robert Lewis Fowler

Alabama & Tennessee: Camp Rucker, 1943-44

Winter Maneuvers

We were in San Luis for only a short period. We shipped out to Camp Rucker, Alabama, for retraining as a new triangular division and to bring everyone up to the status necessary before going to Tennessee for winter maneuvers. We were in Tennessee the last part of November, all of December, and most of January 1944. The maneuvers were very realistic. Five days a week we would be "tactical," i.e. operating as we would in combat. We could not have fires to keep warm. We slept on the ground, many times without blankets. During the day we carried our combat packs, which included only our toilet articles and emergency field rations. Our bed rolls were at the rear and theoretically were to be brought up with the kitchen trucks under cover of darkness. Trouble was, it didn't happen that way very often. Most all of us developed colds at the start. However, when the colds cleared up, it seemed we had developed an immunity; and from then on, we were able to take the worst of conditions.

In one instance we were in a tactical situation where we were to provide cover for the main body as it withdrew. We needed to wade a stream about 50 ft. wide and waist deep. Most everyone waded across as they were. I stripped from the waist down and carried all my gear and clothing shoulder high through the water. Then I was able to put dry clothing back on after the chilly crossing. I got the idea from an old frontier story I had read earlier. Later that night, we had to hold a position and also try to rest. The temperature was just above freezing, and those people with wet clothing and boots suffered miserably. Most of them had to keep moving to get any relief because this was one of those times when our blankets and bedrolls failed to join us.

While crossing the Cumberland River at night during these same maneuvers, we used small flat-bottom assault boats that held about a squad of men. The boat that Sergeant John Cantoni was in capsized when one of his men panicked. The river was slow moving but very deep. Sergeant Cantoni made sure all his men got back to shore by personally guiding them and encouraging them. The heroic thing was, John could not swim. He realized that our winter coats and packs provided some buoyancy for a little while. No men were lost, but there are still a half dozen M1 rifles at the bottom of the Cumberland. Captain Lassiter recommended Sergeant Cantoni for the Soldier's Medal. I don't know whether he ever received it, but he certainly deserved it.

One of the nicest things about the maneuvers was a weekend pass to Nashville. I was able to look up Paul & Lillian Halligan, who lived in Nashville. Paul was in the Air Force. They were old friends from back in Omaha. In addition to their wonderful hospitality, sleeping on their couch, keeping warm, and having a nice hot bath were almost an out of this world experience for me. Our only baths in the field were out of a steel helmet, close to a fire, out in the open. This could only be accomplished on weekends, when we were in a non-tactical bivouac. Five days a week were tactical. No fires. No smoking at night. No loud talking. Digging lots of slit trenches. All this required (taught us) discipline of the highest order.

During all the tactical operations we were accompanied by umpires who wore white arm bands. We were either red or blue, depending on what part of a particular "problem" we were involved in. The umpires were officers and NCOs from non-involved units. They were rotated between units every so often and made continuous reports, either good or bad. Of course, there was a scoring system. Company L was commended several times, mostly for outstanding discipline.

During maneuvers, the weekends were spent in non-tactical bivouac, which was always a timbered area. We would make fires then, and our tents or "fart-sacks" were set up in a circle around the fire. Most of us chose to set up the sack arrangement. As always, we set up in pairs, and the common joke was who was going to be the Mama. We would gather a lot of soft evergreen tree branches for a mattress, lay one shelter half over them and peg down one side. Then we would button the other shelter half as though to pitch a tent, but we would lay it out flat away from the first shelter half. During this time, we each had been issued two more wool blankets, and we would spread all eight blankets over the first shelter half then fold the second shelter half over the top of the blankets. Then the pair of us would remove our shoes and jackets and slide between the blankets—four beneath and four on top. We put wood stakes in the ground near our heads and placed our field jackets over the stakes. We left one side open to let fresh air in, and we used our combat packs for pillows. Our combined body heat helped us keep warm. Sometimes we woke with a few inches of snow on us, but the "sack" did enable us to get a couple good nights of sleep.

During our weekends someone would invariably scare up a rabbit, and you would hear the hunting cry, "Get that Rabbit!" The animal would run in one direction until it came upon another group of trainees, and again the cry could be heard through the timber. The groups were only about 30 or 40 yards apart but scattered over several acres, and you could hear that yell, "Get that Rabbit!" for as long as the poor rabbit had strength to run. Later on, the battle cry "Get that Rabbit" was used almost as much as "All Hell Can't Stop Us," which originated in the Philippines and was supposed to be the official one for the regiment. We almost had another saying that became very much part of our identity. We jokingly told people that *La Wi La His, as* shown on our regimental insignia, meant "We move on Sunday." It seemed that every time we ever made a permanent change of station it was done on a weekend. (I hear tell that a few bold fellows interpreted it to mean "We chase pretty girls.")

North Carolina: Camp Butner, February 1943

In early February I was sent on advance detail, along with representatives from each of the other companies. We went by truck to Camp Butner, North Carolina. The camp was located near Durham, and we replaced the 78th Division. We on the advance detail checked out our future accommodations for our respective units. We made barracks assignments for the different platoons and sections.

One of the important things that happened on maneuvers was my reassignment as platoon guide in the Second Platoon of Company L. I had trained Dolan Boggs as my understudy as C&R sergeant and felt he could handle the job. He was part Indian, so I figured it was a natural for him. The move at this time meant promotion to staff sergeant. It was three years I had spent as C&R sergeant. The platoon guide job was the assignment I had before C&R but with the Third Platoon. The difference was that now the guide position called for a staff sergeant.

The time was February 1943, and the Allies had landed in Italy. Ernie Pyle, a well-known reporter and cartoonist, had taken up the cause of the Infantryman. He brought out the fact that we "dog faces," "ground pounders," and "gravel agitators" or "grunts" (if you were Marine Corps) were the ones that suffered the much larger number of casualties. We had by far the poorest living conditions and were paid the least. Largely as a result of Ernie Pyle's writing, rank in the Infantry was upgraded one level. The platoon sergeant became a "tech". The platoon guide and squad leaders became staff sergeants and assistant. Squad leaders became buck sergeants, and PFCs went to corporal's pay, and buck privates went to PFC. Anyone lower was a recruit, and when he got assigned to a unit, he went up one paygrade.

My transfer resulted from my map reading encounter with Colonel Thompson back in Camp Rucker, six months earlier. At that time, I was with Captain Lassiter at a designated point on the map, at which we were to begin a night withdrawal problem. We were on a daylight reconnaissance of the area when Colonel Thompson drove up and told Lassiter that we were in the wrong location. Lassiter looked at me—his map man. I said "We are at the map coordinates stipulated in the training order, Sir."

Colonel Thompson asked me to prove it, which I did by pointing out different terrain features. The Colonel then agreed with me and asked how long I had been a three-striper and then asked Lassiter why it had been so long. Captain Lassiter had not been company commander more than a few months at the time, so he did not realize just how long I had been stuck on one job.

After the map encounter, my next task was to reconnoiter a route of withdrawal for the whole company of men from the point on the map to a location known as the Battalion Assembly Area. The distance, as the crow flies, was approximately two miles. The route involved going through thick timber, a swamp, and around the edge of an open field. I took my compass heading from my map and went over the route I would take that night. When I arrived at the assembly area, I spotted a roll of toilet paper on a jeep, which I conned the driver out of. I retraced my route back to the starting point and, on the way, I wrapped toilet paper around trees every so often as an aid to my nighttime navigation.

Our time of departure was 2200 hours (10:00 PM). We ate supper tactically. This meant everyone moved through the chow line 10 yards apart, the food canisters were spaced 10 yards, and we did not gather in groups while we ate. When it became time to move out there was a light drizzle, and it was cloudy and dark. At the beginning of the route that I had picked, there was a short stretch of level ground under thick trees, and I realized that it was as dark as a room with no doors or windows. My toilet paper couldn't be seen if you held it right before your eyes.

I got my compass out, and we proceeded single file, each man holding on to a strap from the pack of the man in front of him. I knew we would soon have problems because there was a steep bank about 50 yards in from the starting point. When I found it, it was as though the earth had dropped from beneath me. The ground was soft, so there was little chance of injury, but there was a little confusion. Captain Lassiter was a couple of men in back of me, and when he came down the slide he told me to lead on and he would stay there to make sure each man was reconnected to the man in front of him as they passed—all 160 of them.

I knew the azimuth I had to stay on in order to cross a little stream and the swamp area of two to three hundred yards. I walked with my compass in my left hand and felt for trees in front of me with my right, hoping I didn't shake hands with a snake in the process. I finally came through the clearing and around the edge of it to the assembly area. I had come through the swamp at a better angle than I had planned that afternoon. We were also on a time schedule, and we made it right on the nose. That part was pure luck. There was no way one person could have hurried the column or changed the pace in any way.

The following Saturday I was called into the orderly room, and the first sergeant handed me a written formal commendation from Colonel Thompson with Captain Lassiter's endorsement on it. My greatest pleasure, though, was hearing my buddies' compliments and their wonder as to how I was able to "see in the dark!"

Photo: Fowler sleeping after a long march, his maps spread next to him. The regiment's original helmets, which had to be replaced because of their resemblance to German infantry helmets, can be seen next to his feet.

Our time in Camp Butner was spent initially in care and cleaning of equipment. Many inspections took place—the formal type of inspection, i.e., full laydown of all issue equipment items to be in exactly the correct location in the overall display. These were all very tedious and absolutely boring.

West Virginia: February-March, 1943

From Camp Butner we were taken up to West Virginia and lived in the mountains and deep snow. We were issued special boots and equipment so it really wasn't as bad as Tennessee maneuvers. Some people did get lost temporarily, but no real injuries occurred. During one period, it seemed about a month, we were being fed mutton. It was the worst-smelling and tasting stuff that we had ever encountered. No one could eat it. I tried, but the first bite nauseated me. The PX saw a record number of customers looking for any alternative to eat and medicines to treat gastrointestinal issues.

During February and March, all people were given a chance for fifteen-day furloughs. Fifty percent of a unit could be absent at one time. The month of April brought rumors that it was getting close to overseas time. All preparations were pointed toward being POE (port of embarkation) qualified. About this time, Captain Lassiter told me to plan on getting rid of our underground company fund and also appointed Lt. McAllister, Sergeant Cantoni, and me as the committee for a company party.

The official company fund was money derived from PX profits. The exchange was operated and supervised by the military, and each company received their share periodically. The money was to be used for the good of the unit as a whole. This was now to be spent down to an absolute minimum. The underground fund was built up originally when we had our own slot machine in our day room on Catalina Island. We also had our own PX. As a control board we elected two sergeants, two corporals, and two privates, and I wound up as secretary-treasurer. We also had a one-dollar per man membership token payment. The intent was that the first three weeks of any month, the money was available as a loan to any member that had an emergency furlough or a verified hardship of some sort. The last week of the month, the balance of the fund was available as five-dollar loans to anyone going on pass, to be repaid on pay day. It was a lot of extra work, but I felt good that the men in the company trusted me enough to elect me to the job.

I gave my books to Captain Jacobs for auditing each month. However, when Captain Lassiter took command, he told me he didn't know of any such fund and didn't want to know of any such fund. They were "illegal" in the Army, but they did help out a lot when someone was caught without funds and had an emergency back home. Later the Red Cross would help, but it involved more detail. In L Company it was the man's word.

When Lassiter told us to set up a company party, he told me to liquidate the "illegal" fund, as it wouldn't be needed overseas anyway. Sergeant Cantoni had a car, so it was no problem getting around and making arrangements. We got an opening at the Washington Duke Hotel in Durham and arranged for a dance band from the 35th Division band. All we needed after the ballroom and band was girls. We went to the Chesterfield Factory and made arrangements with a foreman (woman) to bring about forty girls from her department. All things went together and we had a very successful party. Just about everyone showed. Colonel Thompson accepted our invitation as well.

New Jersey: Camp Kilmer, April 1944

The last day of April 1944, all dependents were sent home. We boarded a train and saw Virginia, the District of Columbia, and Philadelphia, mostly from the poorest areas of those cities. We arrived in Camp Kilmer, New Jersey, for final processing for overseas shipment. Wes

Wright and I went up together and visited Jack Dempsey's restaurant and Greenwich Village. We spent a big share of our time lost in the subway system.

During our time at Kilmer, we made out wills and were asked to designate a place of burial if we had a preference. I chose Prairie Hill at Tarkio. We were introduced to censorship at Kilmer—we were not to seal our letters because the company officers would need to read them. This made it very difficult for us to write our loved ones, and some of the guys just refused to write home. Some of the officers understood and told us to bring our letters to them personally. They would initial them after we had sealed the letter if we did it unobserved.

REFLECTIONS VII.
Beatniks and Hippies
Ted Neill

During my senior year in high school I discovered the writings of Jack Kerouac in the form of *On the Road*. Following that, I devoured *Dharma Bums, Big Sur, The Subterraneans,* and *Tristessa*. I was quickly enthralled with Kerouac and all things related to the Beat Generation. Sensitive, vulnerable, and deeply fond of misfits and outcasts, Kerouac presented a model of emotive masculinity that resonated with me. It was a refreshing counterpoint to the likes of Sylvester Stallone, Bruce Willis, and Arnold Schwarzenegger, pictures of machismo presented to me by Hollywood, in which I could not see a shred of my pimply faced, 125-pound self. Better yet, Jack Kerouac's was even a career I might aspire to: that of a writer. I need only go off to see the world with the same all-embracing love, curiosity, and openness to people, whatever their ethnic background, class, or orientation.

Better still was the fact that while reading *On the Road* in 1995-96, I could recognize towns, landmarks, and roadways that Grampa and I had driven the summer before. I was *already* following Kerouac's footsteps . . . or tire tracks.

Jack became my lodestar. Through him I felt connected to a literary tradition, bound to something vibrant, a movement that pulsed with an energy grounded in the American experience. At least this was what the back covers of the books told me. I took them at their word. Here was the spirit of my citizenry, the thing that made me who I was in the world. The frenetic energy of these—almost exclusively—white men in the face of the stiff, oppressive conformity of the 1950s was heroic (again according to the back cover text). Kerouac and his muse Neal Cassady (Dean Moriarty in *On the Road)* fit into the *grand* tradition of other great literary figures, real and imagined, such as Tom Sawyer, Huck Finn, Jack London, Ernest Hemingway, and Kurt Vonnegut. The Beats and their originality were the progenitors of Rock and Roll, the Counter Culture movement of the '60s and '70s, the Peace Movement, the Sexual Revolution, and (again, if the back covers were to be believed) basically all the things that made life in America vibrant, hip, and cool, from Wayfarer sunglasses to the female orgasm.

This love affair of mine continued well into college. Even during my junior year abroad studying creative writing in England at the University of East Anglia, I was still under the spell of the Beats. I enrolled in a course titled "The American Beats," taught by a thirty-something British professor who wore blue jeans, Doc Martens, and Ray Bans. He looked fifty from his own years of hard living. Not a fan of stuffy formalities, he insisted we call him by his first name, Jed. This was something unheard of to me, used to the Ivy League educated professors back at Georgetown. They were squares. Jed was cool, hip, a rebel. Jed would stroll into class late most mornings, red-eyed, carrying a battered leather tote and nursing a cup of coffee, draped in his vintage leather jacket. He would roll cigarettes on the podium and light up. The students took this cue and did the same at their desks. The classroom would fill with smoke, and class was be conducted in a cloud.

Jed had actually *met* many of the Beats before they had flamed out, dying from drug overdoses, heart attacks, or liver disease. He would regale us with stories of hanging out with them. Jed would chuckle at the outrageousness of Jack Kerouac's unbridled alcoholism. Jed likened the moral abandon of Kerouac's drinking to the in-your-face defiance of Beck's 1994 anthem *Loser* with its iconic refrain, "I'm a loser baby so why don't you kill me."

Drinking until your liver "literally exploded" (Jed's words not mine), as Kerouac did on numerous occasions, was something Jed spoke of in a jocular tone. It bordered on awe. Even though the internal hemorrhages eventually led to Kerouac's death, this was a mark of authenticity. The other students, cigarettes in hand, wearing their own uniforms of vintage corduroy, leather, or blue jeans, jackboots or Converses strapped to their feet, would nod sagaciously. As the only one whose hands were not busy holding a cigarette, I took copious notes. My fellow students' sunglasses failed to hide their glares of disapproval. By my very enthusiasm, I demonstrated my own "squareness." Even Jed called me out once for being a bit of an "organizational" man. A black mark of unhip-ness

Jed would break off his lectures frequently after a funny anecdote, as his laughter would dislodge the tar in his lungs. This led to long coughing jags. The students would wait, flicking their ash. My eyes would water.

My disillusionment with the Beats began that semester. It grew as I read the analyses by women writers who had known them, such as

Carolyn Cassady (wife of Neal Cassady of *On the Road* fame) and Jan Kerouac (Jack Kerouac's daughter). The Beats had even included some of these women in their stories, but never mentioned that they, too, were writers. Instead these women were depicted in limited, often sexualized ways. Their talent unrecognized, their inner lives left blank.

The accounts of Kerouac written by his daughter Jan were particularly heartbreaking. She witnessed more than one of the "spectacular" explosions of his liver. Her father coughing up blood into toilets, sinks, and on one occasion, his shirt and hands while on a college campus for a guest lecture, was less authentic than horrifying to a little girl who just wanted her father to *live*.

Disillusionment was further fed when Jed was able to invite Carolyn Cassady to campus. Carolyn had appeared in *On the Road* as "Camille."[11] Even though she had been married to Neal Cassady,[12] Carolyn had been a lover of Jack Kerouac, the affair encouraged by her husband. Over glasses of wine and copious cigarettes with us in the campus pub after class, Carolyn suggested that Jack had been scarred by his Catholic upbringing. This made Jack sexually inhibited and led to further self-loathing, as she also imagined Jack might have been a repressed bi-sexual. Jack also had been wrecked by the "tear-it-all-down" mentality of the Beat Generation—a marketing ploy Carolyn insisted was simply invented by Allen Ginsberg as a way to promote himself. She insisted Jack had simply always been just a poet "in love with the glory and beauty of the world."

Carolyn was fascinating. She was an artist and writer in her own right. She had been sadly neglected by critics and scholars for her male contemporaries (most of whom she ended up burying). But that night in the pub with her, even the gauzy light she tried to preserve Jack and Neal in felt uncomfortable and too kind . . . even for her. It came off as the revisionist memories that one politely presents when confronted with the dissonance of hangers-on and sycophants like Jed and ourselves. We were starry-eyed fans worshiping the Beats and Carolyn herself, not for her own work, but for her association with men who were emotionally neglectful—at best—and abusive, at worst. In the process, I fear we ignored the emotional torment they had caused her. Had she even shared it in a more forthright way, I wonder if we would have had eyes to see it and hearts to hear it.

---

[11] Evelyn Pomeray in *Big Sur, Desolation Angels, Visions of Cody* and *Book of Dreams*
[12] Dean Moriarty in *On the Road*

And the way Carolyn was forced to hold space for both those conflicting visions in her mind, where the men of her life were at once heroes and failures, felt familiar.

It reminded me of my mother and Grampa.

So did Jan Kerouac's plight as a daughter pained by the chaos and suffering of her father, Jack. Carolyn had experienced the same with her husband. Neal Cassady—this "American Hero"—left her a single mother more than once. She had to fend for herself, uncertain if he would ever return, taking welfare and working multiple jobs while Neal disappeared on road trips with Jack and other women, or into prison, or (later) on the endless road trips with Ken Kesey's Merry Pranksters. Neal claimed, always, to be seeking some transcendent meaning, some illuminating breakthrough, some splendid revelation . . . that always proved to be just around the *next* corner. Enlightenment was increasingly elusive as he aged. He ignored the demands of married life, fatherhood, and even the limitations of his body.

Neal Cassady would eventually flame out too, dying from a combination of exposure and renal failure. He was found passed out next to train tracks after a night of drinking and drug use in San Miguel de Allende, Mexico. He slipped into a coma and died just a few days short of his forty-second birthday.

In this respect, it was hard not to see my heroic Beats dancing in the streets professing to be "white negros" as nothing other than white men riding on their privilege and coasting on the post-war affluence of the 1950s and '60s. What was glorious had become grotesque. At the risk of echoing old, haranguing Paul Harvey, I'd say that in modern parlance the Beats would be considered emotionally stunted, dead-beat dads.

Ethically, they were moral disasters. The triumph of their movement felt overshadowed by their messy lives, tragic deaths, and the emotional pain left to their families. It left a sinking feeling in my gut. Despite their contribution to American literature and culture, despite the glowing back cover text crafted by professional marketing teams in New York, I couldn't shake the sense of having been duped.

I've seen videos on YouTube from the 1960s in which Viet Nam War protestors confronted World War II vets who faced them down, in uniform, having come as counter-demonstrators to anti-war marches. The hippies with their peace signs, flower-power shirts, and braided hair are a striking contrast to the military men, many of whom were WWII vets and still enlisted. Their faces were clean shaven, their hair cropped short. They were a far cry from the graying, potbellied World War II vets I had met in the VFW halls. In the 1960s these men were still hale and square-jawed. They were lean and broad shouldered. At that point in their lives, a bit of silver in their hair just added to their gravitas.

The vets faced off with their opposites, sometimes even their children, who donned psychedelic tie-dye shirts, candy-colored sunglasses, frayed shorts, and poorly fitting tank tops. The protestors, those wild members of the Boomer Generation, were declaring their own independence from their parents. They were forgoing bras, shaving, and showers. The veterans on the picket lines were red faced, their eyes ringed in white—if they went as far as to remove their obsidian aviator sunglasses at all. Their rage was spit flecked and full throated. In contrast, the peace warriors were serene. They smiled back with dilated pupils and soft, insouciant grins. I can see how their parents found their cannabis-induced sanctimony hard to bear.

I imagine in the 1960s I would have been in tie-dye, protesting the Viet Nam War as an imperialistic blunder too. But after reading the memoirs of veterans and the scholarship of Edward Tick, I have a growing compassion for those counter-protesting vets and their vehement antipathy towards the generation of Boomers.

The Boomers, as far as their parents were concerned, were naïve, spoiled, and entitled. This echoes the perennial criticisms of *every* generation about the one after. But it's also worth noting how members of Gen X and Millennials resent the Boomers for some of the same things. Born in 1978, I sit smack-dab between Gen X and Millennials.[13] I've heard peers, older and younger, blame Boomers, *their* wars, *their* lifestyle, *their* unbridled consumption, for leaving us fewer resources, fewer opportunities, and a legacy of environmental degradation.

So it goes, as Kurt Vonnegut would lament. So it goes.

---

[13] Some demographers and anthropologists have labeled my cohort, born in the years of 1977 to 1983, as a transitional one—Xenials—exhibiting shared traits of Gen X and Millennials, but unique unto ourselves. We grew up with an "analog" childhood but as "digital" teens, understanding card catalogues as much as the internet. We remember rotary phones, plugged into walls, but also the early years of social media.

Grampa, and Tick, helped me to reevaluate the near-hysteric rage of the vets facing down their stoned children. It was born of their own displaced pain, born of loss, born of trauma. These angry fathers, counter-protesting in their uniforms, were protesting their own lost youth. They were mourning it even, with anger because that was the only emotion sanctioned to them by the era's codes of masculinity. As younger men, they had seen their brothers and their friends make the ultimate sacrifice. They had put their own lives on the line when called to. Through their eyes, I finally understood the disdain and contempt they held for Beatniks and hippies. My own disillusionment with the Beats and their shirking of responsibility contributed to this.

To me, the space between the Greatest Generation and the Boomers seemed to grow wider and deeper, in to a chasm not a gap. These soldiers, whom I could watch dispassionately, decades removed, on YouTube, had seen things their "ungrateful" Boomer kids could not imagine. The smoke of the battlefield was a far cry from the clouds of cannabis smoke hovering over Woodstock. For these men, veterans shouting at their children, their neighbors' children, the sights and sounds of battle were as fresh as their last nightmare. Where the hippies had the Summer of Love, these men had the sweltering June, July, and August of the Normandy invasion, followed by a brutal winter full of trench foot, trenches drenched in blood and shit, all under the screaming shells of German 88s. These were intrusive memories they could not banish, summoned back with searing clarity by something as mundane as the blast of a firework, the backfiring of a car, or the smell of meat on the barbeque that reminded them of burning human flesh.

Tick explains that these veterans felt conflicted, even if they had yet to find the language to say so. Aside from their trauma, they were weighted with a sense of disbelief: why would these children of theirs refuse a call to arms when they themselves had answered with such unwavering faith? This disbelief mixed with a sense of envy, for when these vets were young and learning to love the world, they had to go "shoot at it," as Erich Maria Remarque, the poet and author of *All Quiet on the Western Front,* lamented. There was a sense of deep resentment too, hurt even, on the part of these vets. They had made their choice to go off to war, they had endured the mental, physical, emotional, even spiritual pain of it. Now their own children turned their backs on them. They took their parents' sacrifice for granted. Worse, some Boomers lumped all military service in the category of immoral, imperialistic oppression. Parents found their own children were blind to them, the honor they had tried to live by, and the suffering they still carried.

And the stirrings of self-doubt among these vets were hard to bear, too. Wasn't military service inherently, unquestionably good? They had been raised to believe in its merit, but as later generations do, their children were reexamining this assumption. And as with most protests led by young people and students, it's the younger generation that ends up on the right side of history. They would with the Viet Nam war.

But for the WWII vets, it was easier to project rage against naïve youngsters than question long-held beliefs. It was safer to counter-protest than to self-examine. That could lead to self-doubt, which might shake the foundations of their patriotism, their identity, and the justification for their WWII service in the first place.

I sympathize with the brave protestors who risked the ire of their elders to protest an unjust and atrocious war. Edward Tick has written extensively on the psychic and spiritual toll that the Viet Nam War has taken, not only on individual veterans and Vietnamese civilians, but on the national psyches of the US and Viet Nam.

But I feel for those World War II vets too. They saw blood spilled and lives shattered so their children would not. These fathers endured the screams of rockets and men, the scent of charred flesh, and the smell of bloody viscera. . . . They witnessed flashes of mortality that their "ungrateful, draft-dodging kids" would never have to see. And now their kids called them baby killers. They threw coffee on soldiers in uniform on buses, sidewalks, and subways. Returning from Saigon, soldiers would run into airport restrooms, change out of their uniforms, and stuff them into trashcans as not to be recognized as a soldier returning from Viet Nam, their service a mark of shame.

These reflections make me self-conscious of my own years in England, at nearly the same age as Grampa was when he was there. Fifty years before, Grampa had been in Cornwall, preparing for war on the continent. During my time in East Anglia, the weightiest decisions facing me were what to pack for my backpacking trip of Europe on Eurorail; would I go down into Spain after France or cut east to Italy to see Rome, Venice, and Florence, exploring Switzerland and Germany on my return? Do I go to graduate school or Peace Corps? They felt profound to me. *Some* of these decisions would be life changing, but they all fell far short of life threatening.

Those months in East Anglia, my nights were taken up, not with marches, but with poetry slams and storytelling contests at pubs around the town of Norwich. The greatest danger facing us young college students was stumbling over the original cobblestone streets that had survived from medieval times on the account of Norwich never having been bombed during the Blitz.

And so my adolescent glorification of the Beats would flourish for a brief time. I could embody them, dancing in the streets myself, shouting out my own poetry from the proverbial rooftops. Professor Jed stretched this out well into his fourth decade, where he could be dismissive of Kerouac's alcoholism, as it was a sign of his disregard for the oppressive social norms of the 1950s—which were for squares anyway.

After all, those glossy book covers told us Kerouac was an American hero.

But those flashes of mortality, blood even, have stubborn ways of resurfacing. Long-overdue reminders of suppressed agony.

I saw it in the final years of Grampa's life, when his health was failing and those surgical incisions were failing to heal. His enlarged liver, his swollen guts, had to be held in place by plastic surgical netting, the excess fluid draining through a straw into a bag taped to his body. He had been forced to begin to wear diapers under his clothes due to the control he was losing over his bladder and bowels.

Grampa knew his end was not far off. He frequently cornered my father on visits, whether early morning over coffee watching the sun rise or telling stories down in his "mancave" of the basement. Their discussions were often philosophical, even spiritual, as Grampa wrestled with the guilt he carried from what he perceived as his many failures in life. These were also the days when we saw the flashes of the "old" Bob, as he struggled with the humiliations and, at times, agony of his failing body, when we all feared he might have been drinking again.

I remember one ghastly morning in particular. I was visiting Omaha and staying with Grampa and Coco. I was shocked when

Grampa uncharacteristically lost his temper upon discovering the automatic garage door opener malfunctioning. For the first time in my life, I heard him curse and rage—at the door, at the company, and at the man he had paid to fix it. This was a different side of him, and I thought perhaps the entire family's belief that Grampa never cursed was apocryphal.

Already I was trying to warp reality to fit a narrative of him I preferred. Something tamer. Something safer. Something that was still honorable, heroic, and admirable.

Later that same morning, as we went to pick up Coco at the hospital after a routine checkup, Grampa, whom I had always known as a careful driver, even after our thousands of miles crisscrossing the state, ran a red light. Fortunately, traffic was light and the car coming opposite honked instead of T-boning us. As we continued, I ascribed our drifting in the lane to Grampa's health challenges and the discomfort he was feeling. That was what was interfering with his concentration, I told myself.

I had only known Grampa as sober, and it was indicative of my own denial that, even in the car with a drunk driver, I couldn't imagine he was drinking again.

That morning, after the harrowing ride to the hospital, as I sat across from Grampa in the waiting area, I noticed the arm of his chair and the flap of his jacket turning dark. I wasn't sure of the source of the discoloration at first. Even as I began to suspect the worst, I was reluctant to point it out, given his temperament earlier that morning. But it became obvious when he put his hand in his pocket to grab his keys, only to bring them out covered in his own blood.

A nurse caught sight of him before either of us could react. Soon it was Grampa admitted as a patient. The blood was copious, staining the chair, his clothes, and spilling to the floor in a puddle. The hospital workers moved him onto a gurney. Grampa handled it with the calm stoicism of a man who had seen much worse—because he had.

Or maybe his composure was just the haziness of a drunk about to pass out. I don't know. I never will.

That trip out to Omaha was the last time I saw Grampa alive. I can't help but reflect on all that blood—more than I had ever seen— seeping out of his wound, ruining the furniture, painting his hand in shocking shades of scarlet. There it was . . . that gout of red . . . a flash of mortality . . . indictive of wounds that had never healed and that so many had refused to see.

RECOLLECTIONS OF A GI
V.
Robert Lewis Fowler

May 1944, North Atlantic-Ireland

We were trucked down to the piers one night and we boarded the troop carrier, the USS A.E. Anderson. Each deck below the top deck had tiers of stretcher type bunks, five high with about 24″ vertical distance between them. Only two meals per day were served, and beans for breakfast once a week was a tradition. The PX on board sold a lot of candy bars. Cigarettes were only a nickel a pack. Cigars were cheap but not very plentiful.

The trip across the Atlantic took fifteen days in convoy, which meant zig-zagging the course and various rendezvous points. We spent one evening outside Belfast, Ireland, harbor. It was a beautiful sight when the sun was going down. The name "Emerald Isle" is truly appropriate.

We disembarked at Bristol, England, the next day and boarded trains for Cornwall in southern England. Some were sent to an area called Land's End. Company L ended up near Portshaven, and minus the First Platoon, was billeted in a large, stone estate. Each room had three or four double bunk beds with mattress covers filled with straw, same as we had in the old National Guard camp days. The First Platoon, under the command of Lieutenant Greenlief, was billeted over the hill and down on the beach in a pretty nice beach house. They had a little better set-up but needed to hike over the hill to each meal. The countryside was very peaceful, and a person would never believe that war of the worst kind was only a couple hundred miles away.

May 1944, England

Due to the fact we had spent fifteen days onboard ship, with little if any exercise because of lack of adequate training areas, most of our activities now consisted of walking about the countryside. We started out with two and a half miles for four hours each morning. The platoons alternated leading out and planning the route so that each day we went one mile farther than the day before in the same amount of time. We were doing this on blacktop with combat pack, steel helmets, and individual weapons. We were issued live ammo in case we were strafed by German aircraft. One day, while on one of our hikes, we were having a ten-minute break and we heard a weapon fire one round. It was in the Third Platoon, and one man had shot himself through the ankle. No one ever knew whether it was accidental or not.

During the afternoon hours, if we did not have training films or special schools, we had competition. The Second Platoon organized a football team. Lt. Dailey, Sergeants Ryan, McManaman, and I were the backfield, and we had some pretty big guys up front in the line. Mac had played T-formation quarterback at Holy Name High School; Ryan and I had been reserve halfbacks at Tech High; and Dailey had played in Hastings. Dailey was only 5'7" and 140 pounds, with the biggest feet on a small man I have ever seen. He also was very fast. Ryan and I ran interference for him to get him past the line, and he could g...o...o!

We had some hot competition from the First Platoon. Lieutenant Greenlief had played fullback for Nebraska University, and we knew he was the key to their success, so McManaman and I concentrated on hitting Greenlief every play when we were on defense. Our system worked well most of the time. However, John Cantoni, who was platoon sergeant for the First Platoon, was also very fast, and we had to keep him covered too. We did manage to beat them most of the time.

During one of our hikes around the countryside, word came that the invasion had taken place in Normandy, France. June 6, 1944, was just another day until then. We knew it was just a matter of time till we would be mixed up in it.

I was sent to a couple of schools, each one just a few days duration. One was for understudying as first sergeant. I learned how to make out a morning report and the abbreviations that were to be used. One was "KIA"—killed in action. Platoon sergeants were not to put KIA after a name unless they had personally seen the body. Otherwise it was to be MIA. The other school was about beach landings, disembarking over the side on rope ladders, and enemy combat habits. We learned that, contrary to some older tactics, the Germans were known to have set up defensive positions on the reverse military crest, causing attacking troops to be sky-lined as better targets. We were cautioned that after taking an objective or stopping for any reason you could expect a counterattack within ten minutes. This made it necessary to always know the status of supply or resupply. On more than one occasion I had to inventory and redistribute ammo because some people did not fire their weapon much and others were trigger happy. The ammunition bandoliers were heavy when you carried them crisscrossed over the chest. Add a few grenades and full pouches in the cartridge belt and you were pretty well loaded down. The instruction we received at the various schools was to be passed on to our units when we returned to them. This, of course, was accomplished and hashed over many times.

Sometime after "D-Day" and before we started moving toward the harbors, we received word that Generals Eisenhower and Patton would be coming for an inspection of the 35th and that L Company was picked as the 134th sample. I was disappointed when told that I was to be the temporary CQ (Charge of Quarters). This was normally supposed to be a three-stripe sergeant assignment, and a four striper was not to be used, but the "old man" said he wanted someone who was not afraid of generals, and it was almost certain they would show up to look over our quarters. The generals didn't care about looking at our quarters. They knew that the Company was running live-fire platoon problems, and it turned out that my platoon was going through the attack phase when the inspection party arrived. I never did get to see any of them, and I had to impersonate a lower rank to boot.

June-July 1944, The Channel

We received word to make our vehicles operational while temporarily submerged. This was done with some putty-like material and extension pipes to the exhaust, a snorkel breather for the carburetor, and covering all the ignition items with the non-conductor sealant. It was necessary because we were to land at Omaha Beach, where there were no docks to land on, and we would have to wade ashore in most cases.

We were all ready to go, and on July 1, 1944, we loaded up and moved out to the staging areas near Plymouth and Falmouth. We stayed in tent cities overnight and boarded ship the next day. In the movie "The Longest Day" there are a couple of short scenes showing a chow line in the rain and a tent city. I can attest to the authenticity. We boarded a Liberty Ship, vehicles on the lowest decks and personnel on A and B decks and nothing on the top deck. We were issued "Ten in One" rations (one day's rations for ten men), and they were spread out accordingly. Someone noticed there were steam pipes running alongside the bulkheads, and we put our rations on the pipes so the food was heated and much more palatable.

We were allowed to go top deck and watch all the activity in the harbor and the anti-aircraft balloons as well as other protective efforts for the convoy. We moved out into the channel to a rendezvous area as soon as we were loaded. Some of the guys stayed below deck and started a crap game on a GI blanket. It kept going for a long time, until one guy had most of the L Company's gambling money. I heard it was $1,300, which in those days was a bundle. Most of the guys had their money sent home except for a little cigarette and beer money. I had $90 worth of French invasion money on me, but it was the money that had been collected on payday for the "special" company fund. I had only about $10 of my own money . . . but then gambling never did interest me.

Crossing the English Channel was uneventful.

REFLECTIONS VIII.
Cross Country
Ted Neill

Grampa was anything but a braggart. His war stories were unfailingly characterized by a self-effacing humility, as I was reminded when I called him from a gas station phone in the middle of Kansas, in June 2000.

I had just graduated from Georgetown University with my BA in English and Writing at the end of May. The very next morning I hopped on a plane to join nine other Georgetown students on a cross-country bike ride from San Francisco to Washington, DC. We were raising money for organizations that supported children affected by and infected with HIV/AIDS.

The ride was the idea of Mordecai,[14] an enthusiastic, idealistic, and charming polysexual junior who was deeply conflicted about his sexual orientation and alarmingly narcissistic. Mordecai had been charismatic to persuade us to ride over 3,500 miles, through blazing deserts, grueling mountains, windswept prairie, and humid lowlands. He had talked us into braving roaring semis, less-than-enlightened people throwing everything from beer cans to fireworks at us from moving cars, and dogs—so many goddamn dogs—chasing us and biting us in backwoods enclaves. Mordecai had also been successful at securing donated bikes, food, and supplies for the trip. He attracted media attention, and even got himself invited to the White House. But once on the trip, Mordecai had abandoned all the logistical details of the trip to his longsuffering and overworked roommate and best friend, Thaddeus.[15] While Thaddeus poured over maps, located gas stations, and worked the phones to ensure we had hotels and campgrounds, Mordecai cut a swath through the female riders, sleeping with one after another. Thaddeus, already tasked with riding 100-120 miles per day with the rest of us, got little sleep. He lost weight. Thaddeus also had the unlucky chore of driving an additional 100 miles in a support vehicle (after biking as much) in the evenings to come get me after I became lost—more than once.

Mordecai continued to sow discord among the female riders and awkwardness amongst everyone else as he became infatuated with

---

[14] Name has been changed.
[15] Name also changed.

Thaddeus too. This was betrayed by his uninvited "keyholing"[16] of Thaddeus whenever he bent over. Mordecai was also working furiously on a screenplay in which two thinly veiled stand-ins for himself and Thaddeus led a charity ride across the US, in the course of which they discovered their undisclosed love for one another. It included a series of increasingly graphic sex scenes set in tents and campgrounds—a sort of *Brokeback Mountain* but with bikes.[17]

Needless to say, by the Rockies the ten of us were a feuding mess. By Kansas, I had become lost and separated from the pack a total of three times (still . . . it wouldn't be the last). Lost and waiting at a gas station for Thaddeus to pick me up—again—I called Grampa. I spared him the details of the reality-TV-like mess I had landed myself in. Instead I asked him, "How did you ever lead forty-two men of your platoon into enemy fire and hardened fortifications full of Nazis trying to kill you when I can't cooperate with nine undergrads to ride from point A to point B . . . in peacetime?"

Grampa's answer was typical, provided in understated, self-effacing, and simple terms. Sadly, print does not capture the long pregnant pauses characteristic of his manner of speaking. But he gave a chuckle, either at my high-strung self and my situation, or maybe even himself. "Well . . . I'm not sure. . . . I don't know if I wouldn't have cut and run myself if I hadn't been looking out for the men under me."

It was and wasn't the answer I had expected. Having grown up with a certain image of the military hero, as depicted in *Top Gun* and *Rambo,* I guess I had expected some tough-as-nails talk about knuckling down on your fear, steeling yourself for battle, and "manning up." Maybe I had even been hoping for something like the stirring speeches depicted in films with a background of swelling orchestral music. These were delivered by the actor-of-the-moment, whose character would provide a stirring pep talk in the locker room at halftime to their players. It would be the turning point as their team struggled to come back from a disastrous first half and a deep deficit of plays and points. These were coaches depicted (in rotation) by the

---

[16] Use your imagination.

[17] Thaddeus and Mordecai's friendship did not survive the ride, much less any chance of a relationship, especially since Thaddeus was decidedly straight. Few of us ever spoke to Mordecai again, even as he went on to a successful career as a public relations director for a number of charities and charitable causes where, to this day, he rubs elbows with the rich and famous.

likes of Gene Hackman, Denzel Washington, Sean Astin, James Caan, Billy Dee Williams, Al Pacino, etc. . . . I admit I had hoped for a speech that I could crib and repeat when Thaddeus picked me up and we returned to the campground where the rest of the riders were resting before the next day's ride.

In my own naïve grandiosity, I pictured myself salvaging and "saving" our ride from disaster. Really, I had fallen into the same narcissistic trap as Mordecai, centering myself as hero/leader of everything.

Grampa knew better. Real life, not movies, had taught him as much, but I didn't have a word for the style of leadership he embodied. I wouldn't until I met my other mentors, Steve Olson and Jack Hoban, a decade and a half later.

RECOLLECTIONS OF A GI
VI.
Robert Lewis Fowler

July 1944, Omaha Beach

However, when we neared Omaha Beach we could hear the big guns inland a few miles. We were wearing wool underwear and resin impregnated clothing (for water proofing) for the crossing and landing. It had been a month since D-Day, but there were still body parts floating in the water. We disembarked over the ship's side using the rope net ladders and wearing full packs and the protective clothing. We off-loaded onto a flat barge which moved us to within 50 yards of the beach. Then we waded in. I stepped aside to let my platoon off and stepped into a hole that put the water over my head and my rifle on the bottom of the bay. I dove for it and retrieved it, filled my non-waterproof watch with salt water, and proceeded to shore.

During our trip across the channel we had numerous air raid drills. This meant when the signal sounded the people on the deck had to go down to A deck ASAP. There were ladders at each end of the holds. Each deck floor was a series of removable panels to permit loading or unloading of the lower decks. There was also a removable section around the bottom of the ladders in the end of each hold. During one of the air raid drills, Tom Ryan fell through one of the openings down about 25 feet to the deck where the jeeps were stored. He landed on the canvas top of one of the vehicles, his left shoulder across a metal bough supporting the canvas top, and wound up with a broken collar

---

bone. It was truly the luck of the Irish he was not killed.

This meant that I would take over as the platoon sergeant. Captain Lassiter permitted Ryan to stay onboard ship and be treated by our own medics, rather than be sent back to a hospital in England. (At Ryan's request, Lassiter assigned him as first sergeant of the barracks bag crew). After we were off-loaded, the barracks bags were moved and handled by the Service Company and their two-and-a-half-ton fleet. The bags were kept in a regimental concentration area near the kitchens for all the companies of the regiment, several miles behind the lines.

After reaching the beach, we assembled into company formations and carried our gear, including our barracks bags, up from the beach to an assembly area a couple miles inland. At this time, we removed our impregnated clothing, the long wool underwear, and the fatigues, which were supposed to protect us from mustard gas. We smelled pretty bad after that short hike carrying duffel bags with all that clothing on the 5th of July. We were instructed to put on our "B" uniform, which was wool OD shirt and trousers. Guess fatigues looked too much like the German uniform. Then we were told to turn in our gas masks—which came as a surprise to all of us. In addition to having trained with these things and worn them during off-duty hours for three years and having spent four days wearing the lousy impregnated clothing in July, we were told we didn't need them anymore. It seems British intelligence knew where all of Germany's gas depots were located and could give us at least 24 hours warning before any gas attack could occur. We were glad to get rid of them, but it was very difficult to understand the earlier misinformation.

July 1944, Normandy France

After getting into more comfortable and seasonable clothing, we turned in our duffel bags and gas masks and formed up and moved out. By this time the rumbling of the big guns was becoming more noticeable. We moved into an assembly area about five miles north of St. Lo. It was difficult to find wooded areas for concealment in the terrain we were in, but thank goodness we had air superiority and the Luftwaffe didn't dare show up during daylight. But our Air Force did not dare show up over Normandy after dark. Not because of the German Air Force, but because of our Navy gunners in the channel and anti-aircraft in the area, both Allied and German. Our anti-aircraft gunners fired first and identified the aircraft when they hit the ground. Consequently, Allied tactical aircraft was grounded at 11 PM till dawn.

This gave "bed check Charlie" free reign. Some areas in the Normandy pocket would get flares dropped on them and Stuka dive bombers would work us over a little. Service Company got hit one night, and there were a few casualties but surprisingly light compared to the number of bombs dropped and the noise they made. It is a pretty helpless feeling to be under an air attack. About the only defense is a deep hole.

Photo: Fowler, second from left, looking up, digging trenches with members of L Company shortly before the attack on Hill 122.

July 8th-14th, Villiers-Fossard

On July 8th, the Second Battalion moved into a defensive position to relieve part of the 30th Division for a couple of days then was withdrawn. The 134th was actually in Corps reserve. We had been assigned to the XIX Corp – First Army, commanded by Lieutenant General Omar Bradley. On the night of July 13th, just after dark, we formed up to move out. As we went by the kitchen truck we emptied our pockets of billfolds and anything that would identify where we came from. My wallet contained the $90 that belonged to the L Company special fund, and it was the last I

ever saw of any of my possessions. I was told
later that the mess sergeant had a hell of a
good time in Paris after it was liberated.

Those of us in the Third Battalion moved into
the line to relieve what was left of the 115th
Infantry Division. The 29th was a National Guard
Division from Maryland and Virginia known as
the "Blue and Gray." They were a good outfit
and had been chosen as one of the divisions to
make the initial landings at Omaha Beach. The
First Division (Big Red One) and the 29th were
landed on Omaha Beach on June 6th. The 29th had
been in the line since D-Day and was exhausted
and worn down terribly. Our Third Battalion
moved in and took over their forward positions
at Villers-Fossard, a little village about
three miles from St. Lo. Our positions looked
up toward Hill 122.

Hill 122 will forever be etched in the memories
of all the men that served overseas and entered
combat with the 134th Infantry. Moving up to our
positions and taking over from the 29th on the
night of July 13, 1944, is the date all of us
in the Third Battalion will remember. It
started as we moved out, single-file past the
chow truck. The mess sergeant was standing
there holding a gunny sack, and we were told to
put our wallets and any letters, etc. in it.
Everything but pay card, dog-tags, and
handkerchief. Prior to our move out that night,
Regimental Commander Colonel Miltenberger had a
meeting with all senior sergeants. He told us
how much everything depended on us and passed
on some combat tips that had been related to
him by people who had already experienced
combat.

After the meeting, the squad leaders in my
platoon gave me one of my most cherished

moments when they came as a group to tell me they were glad that I was platoon sergeant and of their confidence in me. I hope they felt the same way after combat. Two of them were killed in the next three days, and all the rest were wounded by the time we made it into St. Lo on the 18th. There were times later when I sure needed someone's encouragement because things happened in combat that the uninitiated cannot possibly conceive or imagine.

The move up was rather quiet. No one talked much, if at all. Each one of us had our own thoughts of family going through our heads, wondering if we would ever see them again. My greatest fear was that I might not be able to control my fear. I was not alone with this. We all had our pride and self-esteem, and to lose it in the eyes of our buddies was as bad as death. We did have a few people who did go completely berserk. Some even shot themselves in the foot to avoid actual combat. I can't imagine how they could live with themselves afterwards, but the instinct for self-preservation can take many forms and overcome reasonable behavior.

We moved into a forward assembly area and spread our men out so that no one was closer than ten yards from anyone else. This was being "dispersed," as called for in field manuals. The idea is that no one round of artillery or mortar fire will cause more than one or two casualties. Needless to say, there was no smoking. I had learned to chew tobacco, and it was a good substitute. Any lights or unnecessary noise could cause us to be shelled. It was a known fact that a lighted match or cigarette would be put out with a .30 caliber bullet, maybe even fired by a friend.

FINDING ST. LO

After the troops were dispersed, and I knew where my squad leaders and platoon leader were, I looked around for the Third Platoon. My closest friend, Leo Samson, was the platoon sergeant of the third. We knew we might not see each other for a while, and possibly never, so we felt compelled to get together to wish each other luck. We had hung out since we were thirteen years old, having met in 1934, and we knew each other as well as brothers. We had shared most all the things life had to offer, and now we were facing something that was truly overwhelming. We did satisfy each other that we were at peace from a religious standpoint, and we knew "there were no atheists in foxholes." Someone had scrounged some cognac and others some wine, and it was being passed around sparingly. No one was about to take more than a couple swigs, for obvious reasons.

Before we had left the States, the Second Platoon received a new platoon leader. His name was Lou Dailey from Hastings, Nebraska. He had originally been in G Company 134 and had gone to the Aleutian Islands with the old Second Battalion. After some time up there, he was allowed to go to OCS and was commissioned a second lieutenant. He wasn't a very big guy, but he was wiry and intelligent and was liked by all. He spent quite a bit of time as an enlisted man, so he had the leadership qualities we respected.

One of our first actions before moving up was to remove our sergeant stripes, and the officers muddied the bars on their helmets. Officers had a white strip about an inch wide and 4 inches long, vertically on the back of their helmets, and we NCOs had them placed horizontally. This was our only designation of authority. Our men knew us by voice, so it was no problem. All of this because of the large number of German snipers. They would hide in trees, etc. and wait for leaders as targets. We even eliminated addressing each other by rank or "sir" and, of course, no saluting. Most of us were on a first-name basis, and Lou Dailey was one of us right away.

By dawn on July 14, 1944, we were in the same foxholes the 29th had left from. We had to dig a few because they boys of the 29th were pretty low in strength by that time. They had lost a lot of people on Omaha Beach, and they had to fight their way to the point where we relieved them. They had received replacements several times. But even with replacement, they had tried to take Hill 122 several times, without gaining any ground.

One of my first memorable combat exploits was having to go to the toilet. The toilet consisted of a little hole about six inches deep, to be covered after use. A person feels very vulnerable at half-mast in a squatting position. Some people claimed that they had been shot at in this position, had tried to run for cover and buckle their belt—all at the same time.

Our platoon was deployed in an L-shape position, with one side of the L parallel to a ravine on our right flank. The Lieutenant and I checked each individual position for field of fire, cover, and concealment. We paired up our people and adopted the buddy system. One of them had to lie awake at all times. One of the first things we had to learn was when you have the opportunity to sleep, you should do so. We were in a static defensive situation at the time, and it was rare for us to be so. During the day on July 14th, the commander of the First

Battalion with his recon group was in our area. They were making their plans for the attack on July 15th. The Second Battalion was doing the same thing in I Company's area. The plan was that the First and Second Battalions would move through the Third Battalion on the morning of the 15th in the attack on Hill 122. Hill 122 was the high ground north of St. Lo, and whoever controlled Hill 122 controlled St. Lo. The 134th was to take St. Lo by the 18th of July.

July 15th, Hill 122

The morning of July 15th started a day that will be in the history of the 134th Infantry forever. Whether a military action is noted in history by the number of casualties, the ground gained, or the ammunition expended, those of us who were a part of it feel that at least one of the next three days on the way to St. Lo was the toughest ever. The reason for one day being worse than another depends on the Company a person was a part of and its assignment.

On the 15th, the First and Second Battalions attacked. The First Battalion gained about 1,000 yards. In those days, that gain was fantastic. The price they paid was horrible. Most units had sixty percent casualties by noon, but they were still pushing and proving that "All Hell Can't Stop Us." The casualty rate among lieutenants and sergeants was appalling, but it did demonstrate that they were out there leading their troops in the tradition in which we were taught.

After the First Battalion passed through us, the sound of exploding artillery and mortar shells was a continuous roar. Occasionally you could hear someone screaming for a medic, but most of the time it was too noisy for a voice to be heard.

Lou Dailey and I had a dugout in a hedgerow corner with the door from an old building as a roof with dirt piled on top. Hedgerows provided protection towards the enemy since they were four or five feet above ground level.

Lou Dailey set up a plan for us to alternate moving from flank to flank through our platoon area to let our troops know we weren't in our holes, and also to show them we were concerned about them. This was my first personal experience of having to move around during a time when it seemed there were explosions all around me. We did have a couple of men get hit with shrapnel that came through the openings of their dugouts. Lou and I took turns going from hole to hole until after noon. Just when I got back from one of my turns and had crawled into our dugout where Lou and our two runners were already in place, an 88 hit directly on the other side of the hedgerow that formed the upper parts of the wall of the dugout. The roof with the dirt piled on it caved in on us.

REFLECTIONS IX.
Fox Hole
Ted Neill

One evening while sitting on the porch in Ogallala with Grampa and Leo, I made some throwaway remark about a local politician campaigning porch to porch for an upcoming election. His first name was Nelson. Plainspoken and exceedingly polite, he shook all our hands and stood with his foot propped on the second step of the porch, sliding the band of his own Stetson up off his sweaty forehead. Leo offered him some lemonade and introduced me and Grampa, the four of us chatting more like neighbors than anything else. Nelson never explained what party he was from or even mentioned a single issue or plank of his platform. This lead me to consider the face-to-face with potential voters a complete failure on his part.

I said as much after Nelson thanked us for the lemonade and left. I went on to announce to Grampa and Leo that I thought Nelson was lacking the sophistication and polish needed for success in the blood sport of politics and possibly life. I was all too ready to relegate him into some weaker and useless category of human being.

Looking back on it, I know my comments were less about Nelson than myself—an attempt to seek validation for a certain type of cutthroat ambition being bred into me in the high-income, highly educated suburb of Washington, DC, where I was growing up. Also, as a teen, having been traveling with two "war heroes" for the past week, I know I was also trying to feel out the borders of an acceptable model of manhood. At seventeen, I was figuring out my own way to "be" in the world. Given my overconfident critique of Nelson, I realize I had—prematurely—concluded that I had discerned the outline of what a "real man" was. Having reached this "wise" and "informed" conclusion, I was eager to show off my understanding by pointing out what—I was certain—were all of Nelson's failings. What I was really, desperately, seeking was the approval of these two men and an initiation into a respectful form of masculinity that I thought they embodied.

I should have known I had erred when Leo let out a less-than-muffled snort. I took it as agreement—derision aimed at Nelson as he made his way down the block, stepping over children's toys, lawn sprinklers, and through latched garden gates to, pitifully, shake more hands. For the briefest of moments, I reveled in the satisfaction of having "figured it all out." Nelson was a mild-mannered, middle-aged milksop. I, by contrast, under the mentorship of these two men, was on my way to an invincible, unconquerable manhood. Having been a lean, bullied, sensitive boy growing up, I was basking in the sense of being "one of the men," for once in my life.

And I hadn't hesitated to bully someone else.

But I had it wrong. And, of course, Leo's derision had been for me. But like one good officer who sees another officer's man out of line, Leo let my own commander put me in my place.

Grampa answered after a long pause, my mind already having moved elsewhere.

"You'd be surprised, Ted, who would jump out of a foxhole and run by your side to charge the enemy."

I thought another war story was coming, but it only dawned on me slowly that Grampa was talking about the present. A long pause followed. A few cars rolled past. A lawn sprinkler made a few revolutions. Leo waved at a couple of children catching lightning bugs. Grampa continued, "Guy like Nelson there, he'd be the first one out beside you. You wouldn't have to worry about him hanging behind. He'd have your back."

More to my shame, it wasn't until years later that I realized just how far I had mis-stepped and that this was actually a soft, but firm, rebuke from Grampa. Over time, and since confirmed by reading his memoir, I came to realize Grampa (and Leo's) deep affection for what I, in my East Coast, college-educated snobbery, would have considered "the common man."

Men like Nelson.

Men like themselves.

Having seen so much of human nature, tested in life or death circumstances, Grampa and Leo had more intuition, ability, and right to judge a man or a woman's character and how they might perform under the worst of stress than I did. Even so, they were both slow to pass judgement aloud, a great contrast to me in my teenage arrogance.

Nelson went on to win the election and served in local government for many years. Grampa and Leo had confidence, after interacting with him just a few minutes, that's he'd pass their test of character.

The jury was still out on me.

RECOLLECTIONS OF A GI
VII.
Robert Lewis Fowler

July 15th, cont. . . .

Lou Dailey was almost completely covered, and we all were a little stunned. I had a hot piece of shrapnel, only about the size of a bb, imbedded just under the skin. I dug it out and forgot about it until the point system for wounds came out after VE day.

By this time, the First Battalion had gained enough ground, so we in the Third Battalion moved out to the right flank of the First Battalion.

We were moving over to our right toward the road that leads from Villiers-Fossard to St. Lo. We thought the 320th was on our regimental right and that their left boundary was the road. But, in reality, they were not that far forward, so our flank was open.

We got out to the road and turned left toward St. Lo after some delay. The man I had picked as my second in command was fatally wounded by a sniper. He was still alive when we last saw him. The medics picked him up, and he died a couple of days later.

As we proceeded up the road toward St. Lo, our platoon was leading out with column files on each side of the road. We passed an opening in a hedgerow between the road and a field to our right, and we received enemy machine gun fire right through the opening. It then became obvious that the 320th was not abreast of us on our right flank and that we were exposed.

The battalion commander had me send a squad to try to neutralize the enemy machine gun. "Mole" Owens had a rifle with a grenade launcher, so Colonel Thompson told him to use the grenade on the machine gun. Owens put a live round in the chamber of his M1 and fired. There was supposed to be a blank to propel the grenade to the target. It happened that the Colonel was standing close by, and he and Owens both were splattered with little specks of lead. Their faces looked like they had a pox with little drops of blood. Neither was hit in the eyes. In the effort to eliminate the enemy machine gun, PFC John Quinn was killed with a bullet through the head.

Later we proceeded up the road, and our squad was still involved in a fire fight on the right flank. Wes Wright was shot through the back of his neck, a little to the left of center, and the bullet came out through his right cheek. When I saw him, I thought he was shot through mouth, as he was lying on his left side in a ditch.

About this time a German tank started spacing rounds down along the road. Also, mortars were dropping in the road up and down the column. Everyone hit the ditches, including me. I can't remember how long this lasted, but it seemed like forever.

The shelling finally stopped, and we found that the Colonel and his command group were cut off from the rest of us. We had been bypassed by the command group when we were involved with the machine gun on our right flank. Major Wyant, the executive officer, took command and had us move back down the road and into a field where we could disperse. About dusk, I had to send a squad to Battalion Headquarters to go on a patrol up to where we were, to see if they could find the Colonel.

I had to pick a squad. I had the squad leaders draw straws, although I warned them they would be taking their turn in the future. It turned out to be Ralph McManaman's squad. They returned a couple of hours later and no results. Colonel Thompson and his group were able to crawl their way to safety and return to the Battalion.

July 16th

The morning of the 16th, the Third Platoon led off and we found that some enemy had infiltrated across the road. They were routed and the First Platoon took up the attack. The Battalion moved up to Emilie during the day, after hard fighting by the First Platoon, led by First Lieutenant Greenlief and Technical Sergeant John Cantoni. During that day, their 42-man platoon dwindled to ten. The Germans had the advantage of prepared positions to keep moving back to a supply of ammunition waiting for them. We had to carry our ammo with us, and being on the attack without the help of artillery is as tough as it gets.

At dusk, the First Platoon was holding their position where they had stopped, and the Second was right behind them, and the Third was behind us. About midnight I was called to Company Headquarters and told I would have to lead my platoon with the rest of the company behind it over across the St. Lo road and make contact with K Company. Then we would move into a position ready to attack at 0430, July 17th. We were able to get into a hole and pull a raincoat over the top of us and look at a map by flashlight. This was the first time I had even seen a map since we landed in France.

July 17th

At 0400 I wondered why I ever wanted to be a sergeant or anything else except a buck private. I was to lead what was left of a company of men over strange terrain with plenty of enemy nearby, 200 yards, maybe closer, and what was more, I wasn't reconnaissance sergeant. But Captain Lassiter wanted it this way, and there it was. I made the move and contacted a lieutenant from K Company. They were to be on our right flank and move out the same time as us, at 0430.

There was a ground haze, or fog, and at 0430 it was very dark and quiet. We were to attack without any artillery preparation on the theory that preparatory artillery always acted as a signal for the Germans to harden their defenses in anticipation for a ground attack. We had been surprised at how much machine gun fire the enemy could deliver, even when they were not "prepared." We hoped to catch them by surprise this morning.

Lou Dailey's plan of attack was that he would take two squads forward, and I would follow with the other squad. I was to employ them where I saw fit when I received word from Dailey to do so. After 100 yards or so, the Kraut machine gun opened up. We had run smack into their MLR (main line of resistance). This was where they were to hold ground at all costs. We were suffering heavy casualties, and finally I sent the reserve squad to the left, even though I hadn't heard from Dailey.[18]

During this time, I had one of my launcher men try to launch a grenade on the machine gun position hitting us from over on our right. The problem was, we had been getting some dud grenades, caused by a safety sleeve not sliding back by the time the grenade arrived to target. To compensate, I removed the grenade from the launcher and removed the sleeve. But while putting the grenade back, the safety lever slipped out of my grip. The grenade should have blown, but my finger got stuck between the firing pin and the percussion cap. It was "safe" as long as my finger was in there. Then I had a horrible thought that if I were to get hit, reflexes would cause me to pull my finger out, and I would have to get rid of the grenade in four and a half seconds—if I was still conscious to get rid of it at all. (Four and half seconds is the time the fuse burns after the striker pin hits the percussion cap, which gives time to throw the grenade and for it to arrive at the target.) I couldn't run the risk

---

[18] The casualty rate for Fowler's platoon, the second, were astronomical. Six out of seven men perished. Part of the reason that the German MLR was so difficult to overcome was that the Germans had captured the Allies' battleplan for St. Lo and Hill 122. Even as well-fortified as the bunkers on Omaha Beach were, the Axis countries were still never completely certain if the Allied landing would be from the English Channel or somewhere else in the Mediterranean. This was partly a result of the brilliant counterintelligence work on the part of the Allies, as recounted in Ewen Montagu's magnificent book: *The Man Who Never Was.* As a result of this bold counterespionage, on D-Day the Germans were still somewhat caught off guard. This was never the case for Hill 122 and St. Lo. The Germans were well prepared, deeply entrenched, and reinforced. They had no doubt the Allies were coming, and they knew the stakes: the invasion of Europe and the survival of the Axis powers hinged on St. Lo. In the end, this was why it took thirteen regiments and a terrible cost in lives to take Hill 122 and St. Lo. In the aftermath, "It looks bad, but not as bad as St. Lo," became a common refrain among GIs when sizing up the subsequent devastation and carnage of the European campaign.

of getting hit and dropping the live grenade so close to the other men. I had to get rid of it. I searched for a place to ditch it, found a depression in the ground, and threw the grenade in there. It exploded without harming anyone in the immediate area.

It was after daylight when I received word through Sergeant Lloyd of the Third Platoon that Captain Lassiter had ordered us to pull back. He had seen our wounded coming back and knew we were in bad shape, so he had called Colonel Thompson and received permission to pull back. I Company would replace us and resume attack. We didn't know it at the time, but we had killed a large number of the enemy and could probably have moved forward with the men we had left, but we never gave any thought to it at the time. I crawled up to where Lou Dailey was and informed him of the withdrawal order. He said take the left side and he would take the right and get back any men that were still alive. This took some time, and it was tough finding the men that were killed. I moved back myself to the location where Dailey said to meet him. He was in a shell hole. I could see his head sticking up over the edge. I was standing and yelling about ten yards away that my side was all clear. He started to answer me and I saw his head drop and he went limp. I rushed over to him and saw that a piece of shrapnel had gone through his mouth from the front and had gone through the throat and was in the back of his neck. He bled to death in a matter of a few seconds. His radio operator had been kneeling beside the hole when it happened and didn't get a scratch. I took him with me and reported back to Captain Lassiter. It wasn't long until the usual counterattack came. It was beaten back successfully by our return fire after we got reorganized.

Many of the men were in foxholes behind the original hedgerow that we went over when we started out at 0430 that morning. After what they had been through the last three days, they were reluctant to get up and fire back to stop the counterattack. Lieutenant Greenlief and I immediately started moving up and down the hedgerow, getting the men up into firing position. We did receive a mortar barrage that had us all back in those holes. When it was over, we knew they would be coming, but we were ready, and they never even got close. We picked enough off that they got discouraged rather quickly. It was our turn to fire from a protected position, and they were out in the open on the move.

During this time, I remember one of the men by the name Marion Pennington. He had been mobilized with us on December 23, 1940, and had been in the National Guard before that. His civilian job had been as an elevator operator at the local YWCA Building. He was pink faced and pudgy and lacked the ordinary coordination expected of most men of those days. We had tried several times when we were stateside to get him to take a discharge. He knew he didn't have to and said he joined the outfit to fight for his country, and he meant it.

When I saw Penny that day just prior to the counterattack, he was not one of those we had to pry out of the foxhole to fire back. He had his Bazooka across the hedgerow, and he cussed me because I wouldn't load it for him. I told him that we had to save the ammo in case of tank attack, and I gave him my M1 to use and found myself another. I will always remember his statement that he joined the outfit to fight for his country.

When it came time for us to move out of the position we were in, Captain Lassiter told Lieutenant Greenlief we would need an automatic weapon on the other side of the road that we had to cross and somewhat follow the route we had come a couple days before in order to get back to a covered position to reorganize due to the heavy casualties.

The next thing I knew, Greenlief picked up a BAR (Browning automatic rifle) and hollered "Bob, grab an extra BAR cartridge belt and let's go!" It wasn't an order, just something we had to do. He dashed across the road, and a few seconds later I did too. I was thinking he surprised the Krauts first but they would be waiting for me. The road we crossed went right into the enemy positions, so we expected fire from them. However, what was left of Company L crossed the road on the run, one man at a time; Greenlief and I had set up our gun position to answer any fire we might receive.

As the Company withdrew, Greenlief and I did a rearguard action to cover them until they were all safely back to the reorganization area. We both were glad that the rearguard action didn't require the sacrifice seen in the movies or sometimes during the real thing.

Getting back to the unit and checking who was left was a very painful procedure. Normally an infantry company had 187 men. Subtract seventeen men such as mess sergeant and cooks, KPs, truck drivers, clerks, and you have 170 men on the line. Each rifle platoon has forty-two men and the weapons platoon the balance, except for Company Headquarters which has a first sergeant, communication sergeant, and four runners in the command group.

Lieutenant Greenlief had ten men left in his First Platoon. Sergeant Cantoni, his platoon sergeant, had been wounded earlier that day, rifle bullet through the left lung. He had walked back to the medics under his own power. I had six men left and I had lost Second Platoon Leader, Lieutenant Lou Dailey.

The Third Platoon was not in as bad a shape as the First and Second Platoons, but they were down fifty percent. Both Lieutenant Campbell and my buddy, Leo Samson, were OK.

The Weapons (Support) Platoon had lost its platoon leader. An artillery shell hit a tree above him, and although not scratched, he went berserk and started running around in circles, chasing imaginary enemy. We never heard how he turned out, if ever. Sergeant Jerry Sokol was in charge of Weapons Platoon, and they had their share of casualties, but not near as bad as the rifle platoons.

The First and Second Platoons were combined temporarily under command of Lieutenant Greenlief and me as platoon sergeant. After a few more minor reassignments, we formed up to move out. Our platoon had reorganized in a small field on one side of a road, and the Third Platoon had used a little field on the other side of the road. It happened that I came through the gate out to the road, and there was Leo Samson at the head of his platoon, also coming out. Just a glance and a nod were all there was, but there were a thousand words unsaid.

We headed out up the road back toward the area where we had lost so many men. I started thinking of what I could have done to have saved them, and I had such a sad and remorseful feeling come over me that I started crying like a baby. The company commander thought I might be losing it, but I told him that I just felt such sorrow. I had lost Dailey, McManaman, Tiedje, Quinn, Dick Campbell, Pelegrino, and several others, all these men from my platoon, and some were very close. A sergeant isn't supposed to have close friends in his platoon, but we had been together a long time—some of us for three years.

I remembered a discussion we had back in England before we crossed the channel. It was just we sergeants of the Second Platoon, and we were talking about going into combat. We all expected that, being infantry, we would get wounded at some point. We were naming the wounds we wanted to avoid if possible, in their severest order. First, we didn't want to get killed; next, we didn't want to lose our eyesight; then we didn't want anything to happen to our masculinity; then we didn't want to lose an arm or leg. We would settle for a nice little flesh wound that could be sewed up easily.

We moved forward to a position about 300 yards in the rear of the two Assault Companies, I and K. Then it was digging in until we were told to move up and relieve I Company, which had relieved us earlier in the day. We moved into our position, and then we were told to display our position marking panels. The Air Force sent a recon plane with cameras, and this would give the higher headquarters our forward positions in order to put the finishing touches on "Operation Cobra."

REFLECTIONS X.
Ghosts
Ted Neill

I found, in reading Grampa's story, little moments, oblique references that became loose threads that I followed to a more profound understanding of him and an appreciation for the choices he made. It gave me insight into why his men followed him and trusted him as a leader.

The most telling moment was the choice to hand over his M1 rifle to Private First Class Marion Pennington, "Penny," while under enemy fire. There was something so inherently counterintuitive to it. Giving somebody *else* your weapon? While under fire? What sort of instinct for survival was that?

But on reflection, my lack of comprehension was indicative of my own selfishness, making me realize that I had missed the profound meaning in that lesson Grampa offered me so many years ago on the bike ride—that humble admission that even *he* might have cut and run had it not been for his obligations to his men. As usual, I had failed to grasp the true importance of what he had shared.

Mine was an attitude of self-preservation, Grampa's, self-sacrifice.

The wisdom was also there, hidden in his soft rebuke of me on Leo's porch, after I had dismissed candidate Nelson. Grampa had been trying to help me not to make the same mistake he had: the mistake of underestimating someone else. In Grampa's case it had been the uncoordinated, "pink-faced and pudgy" Private First Class Penny (the Nelson of his era), who had done nothing more glamorous in his previous life than operate an elevator at the local YWCA. Grampa and his cohorts had tried hard to convince Penny to drop out, having come to their own premature opinion regarding the mettle of his character.

But in the line of fire, Grampa saw Penny for who he was: determined, courageous, and heroic. And like a good leader, Grampa gave Penny what he needed, even if it meant more danger for himself.

Steve Olson, my boss at the Center for Ethics and Leadership, and Jack Hoban would stress to me that, in the simplest sense, a leader is the person, man or woman, who *goes first.* This often means risk. The risk can be mild, such as receiving criticism, or it can be severe, such as being shot as the first person out of the trench. Steve Olson would explain to me that, although many people envy the "perks" they see associated with leadership (especially corporate ones), leadership, for many followers, simply amounts to task and risk avoidance—we're actually much happier to let leaders do the hard work, to take the risk of making hard decisions. Then we don't have to. This is especially true when it means being the first out of the trench, the first to be shot at, shot down, and shot dead.

This was the value Steve saw in bringing business and NGO leaders to Quantico to get a taste of the leadership and ethics training Marines receive. Removing civilian leaders from their all-too-safe environments of boardrooms and C-suites and putting them under fire—even simulated—would help them better understand what real leadership was. Real leadership means risk, it means sacrifice, even of yourself.

Not just your own parking space or flying first class.

The term "servant leadership" has been in vogue among leadership coaches, corporate consultancies, and throughout the "leadership" literature. Peer-reviewed journals and New York Times bestsellers extoll its virtues. The concept of servant leadership is not new. Lao-Tzu wrote about it in the *Tao Te Ching*. So did the Indian philosopher Chanakya in the *Arthashastra* around four or five hundred years BCE.

Servant leadership boils down to a style of leadership that—in contrast to traditional notions of top-down authority—puts the needs of others first. The obligation of the leader is to wield power and distribute resources to help others develop to their best ability. The servant leader is successful when those s/he serves, those "under" him or her, fulfill their potential and perform their best. Leadership exists to serve the needs of the followers, to bring them up, to empower and equip them.

Not the other way around.

Centuries later, Bill Wilson, founder of AA, described servant leadership as leadership not "on top" but "on tap," picturing it as a spring or a reservoir for others to benefit from.

In Christian tradition, scholars point to Jesus's teachings to his disciples, specifically in Mark 10:42-45, as an example: "Whoever wants to become great among you must be a servant and whoever wants to be first, must be servant to all."

The concept remerged and increased in popular use as a result of Robert K. Greenleaf's essay, "The Servant as a Leader," first published in 1970.

Done right, servant leadership creates great leaders and inspires men and women to do extraordinary things. But it exacts an emotional toll on the leader who takes its principles seriously, for the leader carries a commitment, devotion, and even love for his followers in his heart. So it was no surprise to me to read how Grampa "cried like a baby" as he returned to a more secure position and realized that out of the forty-two men in his company, only six had survived. His company, going up against the main line of resistance of the Nazis, well entrenched and well prepared and with an understanding of the stakes, had suffered the worst casualties of their battalion.

The Allied generals had determined that it was possible to overcome "static" fortified positions but only by overwhelming them with numbers. This meant high casualty counts reported to HQ in the columns of carbon-copied morning-after-action reports. On the lines, it meant friends, with names not just numbers, dying in your arms. It meant the living carrying the burden of loss and the guilt of survival with them for life.

The grief would never leave Grampa. I think over the decades it just compounded. As I learned in 1995.

While on our trip across Nebraska, Grampa had said to me that even after going to war and losing so many men, after losing his Evelyn to cancer, it had been losing a child that had been worst for him. In 1953, my uncle Mike went into the hospital for a routine tonsillectomy. Something went wrong with the anesthesia, and Michael, at the age of five, died on the operating table.

My mother's lasting image of her father that day was of him weeping in the corridor, clutching Michael's favorite toy. It was a horse figurine, of the brown and white Indian variety. The leg had broken off. Michael had asked his father to fix it for months. Grampa had promised he would, but never did.

That day in 1953, in the hospital corridor, Grampa also cried like a baby, trapped in a hell of his own self-condemnation. He had no words of comfort for any of his reeling children, my mother, my aunt Mary Anne, and my aunt Elyse. They had lost their brother and were reeling themselves. But he was incapable of providing the comfort a father is expected to. Instead, he cried into his hands, holding

Michael's broken horse, saying only, over and over again, "I never fixed it. I never fixed it."

This loss would further manifest in an emotional distance, a cruel coldness even, that Grampa had for the next youngest child, my aunt Elyse. She would grow up on the far side of a chasm of disregard from her father as he kept himself separated in his grief, hence the only time he embraced her was to smother a grease fire.

Later, as Grampa was taking steps towards sobriety, the grief would transform into a doting interest on his youngest daughter and last child, Sally. My mother and the other older siblings saw this as the overcompensation it was. For the first time, after seven previous children, Robert Lewis Fowler changed one of his children's diapers. He was attentive and emotionally available to Sally in ways he had never been to his other children. This left his other children jealous, the resentments emerging in cutting asides and snide digs at family gatherings, even today. I once heard my own mother—after a few drinks—remark to a blindsided Sally that, "I had to change everyone's diapers growing up . . . then you came along and Dad was suddenly *interested* and changed yours."

Evelyn and Bob never thanked my mother, Kathy, even though some of my aunts remember her doing more for them than their own mother growing up. Mom left for nursing school and the East Coast burnt out, determined to never have a large family herself and to never move back to Omaha.

Returning to that scene of Grampa weeping for Michael, though, I can't help but see the parallels between that moment and that day in Normandy, when the counts came in and he knew that eighty percent of the men who had "run out of the foxhole" behind him were dead. I feel some certainty that the tears he wept for Michael were also for those brothers he had lost—surrogate sons whom he felt responsible for, whom when they were struck down by bullets or blasted into pieces by mortars and mines, he could not fix. The trauma of it was likely contributing to his heavy drinking, even then.

And even in old age the pain had not left him. While in France for the fiftieth anniversary of D-Day, Coco told me that at a GI dinner hosted by the residents of St. Lo, during a speech from the current mayor, Grampa's gaze drifted away from the stage to the corner of the room where a few young children were waiting. These were all children of primary school age, whispering and admonishing one another in French, which Grampa didn't speak. But the language between older siblings trying to corral younger ones is universal and timeless. Grampa watched these grandchildren of the French families he and his men had liberated and was seized with weeping once more. Whether he saw his own children, his own comrades, or just a vision of childhood innocence, I'm not sure. I am certain, though, that this was a clue that this return trip to the scenes of battle was not all about triumphalism and victory.

Nowhere was this clearer to me than in the image that came to represent the climax of that trip in 1994. It was the moment Grampa, as one of the few survivors of the fighting on Hill 122, stood before the monument erected in memory of the men who gave their lives to liberate St. Lo. A photographer captured Grampa as he stepped up to the memorial, a wreath of flowers in his arms, his eyes full of emotion, his mouth parted, its corners downturned. He wears the expression of a man overwhelmed with emotion, out of step with the grateful adults and happy children waving small American and French flags in the background. They are cheerful. Grampa is haunted.

The picture would go on to be published across the front page of the Omaha World Herald—the very same newspaper that had breathlessly described the 35th Division's victorious march across France, Belgium, and to the borders of Germany as they defeated "Hitler's Best Troops" fifty years before.[19] The picture of Grampa from St. Lo would be reproduced, framed, and hung in living rooms of family, extended family, and friends. My mother and father hung it next to Grampa's medals after his death. The picture became a lasting, *the* lasting, symbol of his service. Most viewed it as festive and celebratory.

But I never saw it like that and still don't. After reading his memoirs, after reflecting on his life, I see Grampa's eyes now and I recognize, as Edward Tick says, the eyes of a man who, like so many soldiers, carried a cemetery in his heart. Ghosts followed him, whether they were Michael's, or his other son Joe, whom he would also bury in his lifetime, or the men he couldn't save, the lives he could not fix, losses he had no answer for . . . we'll never know. And even after clawing back a few decades of sobriety, banishing those ghosts along with his whiskey and gin bottles, eventually those ghosts would get the best of him again, tormenting him into a drunkard's death.

---

[19] See Appendix

Photo: Fowler in St. Lo, laying a wreath at the monument to fallen soldiers on the Fiftieth Anniversary of the town's liberation.

RECOLLECTIONS OF A GI
VIII.
Robert Lewis Fowler

July 18th

We spent the night in the positions that we took over from I Company. The next morning was July 18, 1944. We were waiting for our resupply of ammo, food, and water, which normally would have been brought up to us under cover of darkness. Since we had received no word as to a reason for no supply, Captain Lassiter feared we might be cut off from the rear. I was told to take a combat patrol of twelve men and go back to get ammo and rations and fight our way if necessary. I was given authority to pick any men from the Company I wanted. I picked Matt Lloyd from Third Platoon and Al Grobe from the First Platoon. The rest of the twelve I don't recall. Lloyd was to be my second in command, and I kept Grobe as my partner since we never operated alone because of snipers. In addition to getting our supplies, the CO wanted me to pick up some gear he had left in a foxhole in our old positions of two days before.

We proceeded back approximately a mile without any problems. We came upon the reason for all the delay in supply. During the previous night, the jeeps and trailers from each one of the rifle companies in the battalion were bringing up our supplies, and the lead jeep, which belonged to I Company, had tried to go around an American tank knocked out by a mine a couple of days before. The I Company jeep also hit a mine and was blown into a pile of torn and twisted metal that defied identification. I saw the body of the driver in a field where it had landed. His intestines were strung out on nearby trees, and his torso was split open from his neck to his crotch. It appeared there was not a piece of bone in his body more than two inches long.

The road they were on was a sunken road with a bank on each side six or eight feet high and also steep. The road level was four or five feet lower than the field level on the other side of either bank, and also trees and bushes grew out of the top of the banks like all the hedgerows in the area. The mine field had to be cleared before the rest of the jeeps could proceed. They were later backed up and rerouted, but this took a lot of precious time.

I immediately turned the patrol over to Sergeant Lloyd and had them take all the supplies they could hand-carry and return to the Company. I kept Al Grobe with me and located the items Jungle Jim wanted and also located some bodies of L Company men that had not been picked up by the Graves Registration people.

We came upon an American soldier from the 320th taking items like watches and rings from the bodies of our dead. I clicked off my safety on my rifle and was prepared to kill him on the spot, but Grobe talked me out of it. The bad part about it was that we had no time to arrest him and turn him in. We had to send him back to his unit and hope he got there in time to get shot by the enemy.

We returned to the Company with no more incidents, except I found an M1 to replace the one I gave Pennington a few days before. I was able to check out the "zero" of the weapon on a suspected sniper position in a tree some distance in back of us. I had some tracer ammo, so I could fire and adjust the sights very easily.

Not long after we returned to the Company, we moved out in the attack. Outside of a few stray rounds of artillery, we didn't have any problems for several hundred yards. Along about 6:00 PM that evening we had stopped to straighten out our formation and organize for one more attack forward. Jake Sass took a patrol down along the road toward St. Lo until he encountered the enemy. He returned and passed on the location where enemy fire had come from.

In the meantime, our position had been discovered by the enemy. We received a pretty tough artillery attack until three Air Force Thunder Birds (P47s) came along and evidently saw the gun flashes of the German artillery. We saw them strafe and bomb, and we received no more enemy fire for quite a while after that.

We formed up for our last assault toward St. Lo. It was the 18th of July, 1944, and we were to have St. Lo without fail on this date. We were to move out behind a rolling barrage of our own artillery.

We had some difficulty getting the guys to move out. They had dug foxholes while we were delayed, and leaving that protection was tough. We all knew what going into the attack meant— marching, fire, and casualties. I looked at the other end of our hedgerow we had to go over to start off our attack, and Lieutenant Greenlief was standing on the hedgerow and waving the men to follow. I did likewise on my end until we got them all moving.

After the men were moving, Greenlief told me to take a couple of volunteers down a sunken trail that was between us and the Third Platoon and parallel to our direction of attack. We knew the enemy could come up the trail and get at our flanks, so we would deny them this and use it ourselves.

I was able to get Gordon Weeks and Bill Bailey with a BAR, and we took off down the trail, firing a few rounds ahead of us, and made good progress. After a while I had to climb a bank to see if we were ahead or behind the attacking platoons. I found that we were OK. Greenlief told me to take over the platoon and have Weeks go down the trail. We were to keep up the attack on into St. Lo, which was just ahead of us.

Once we had gotten the men moving and we were having such good results, we really made progress. When Greenlief had turned the platoon over to me, he had gone back to see how the Company as a whole was doing and found out that we were to stop at the edge of the town and let the 29th Division go on into town from the left and mop up.[20] We had to stop our own people and bring them back to a road that had been designated as a restraining line.

I immediately started to consolidate our position. The goal was to put the men in a position so they could dig in, in an organized manner, and arrange for resupply of ammo. No sooner had I done this than the counterattack came. An enemy machine gun crew had moved in on our flank under the cover of enemy artillery fire, and they played havoc for a while.

---

[20] While the 134th was the first regiment to technically "enter" St. Lo and it took thirteen regiments to take the city, the 134th pulled back to allow the 29th Division to enter first, as it was the men of the 29th who had stormed the beaches on D-Day and had suffered such atrocious casualties then, during the subsequent push inland, and while holding the line at Hill 122 until the 134th came to relieve them.

Sergeant Bill Tombrink and Pat Micelli were killed. Frakes was wounded in the shoulder, and I was able to find a hole the enemy had dug for a gun emplacement, so I was lucky. In the meantime, some of our guys spotted the Kraut machine gun crew and killed them. I spotted a Kraut climbing a tree across the road in an orchard and, although the foliage hid him from sight, the wiggling branches gave him away. I emptied a clip interspersed through the tree and saw no more movement. A hedge in front of me obscured my view of the trunk of the tree, so I didn't see him come down, but a man from our flank saw him. I hadn't killed him, but he was wounded and retreating.

Captain Lassiter told me to take a reel of sound power wire and a phone over to our flank, where the First Battalion was located. This enabled him to relay information to direct artillery fire from our own Cannon Company, which was actually a battery of 105 Howitzers. I would also be able to prevent accidental rounds landing on friendly troops. While on the way over to the other battalion, I was narrowly missed by a round from a sniper that was in our area.

The German counterattack was stopped, and we were finally able to consolidate our position. We proceeded to dig in and improve our positions. I took over a dugout the enemy had used as my own spot to get some sleep once all my men were taken care of.

REFLECTIONS XI.
Life
Ted Neill

There was a further aspect of Grampa's story that I only learned to talk about, much less appreciate, after apprenticing under Steve Olson and Jack Hoban. It is a crucial element of the return journey of the heroic quest and the reintegration of the warrior into society. It centered on the recognition and affirmation of shared humanity, with brethren, with strangers, even with the enemy.

This philosophy (mentioned in earlier sections) called the *Dual Life Value*, is one that Jack Hoban has written at length about in his books *The Ethical Warrior* and *The Ethical Protector*. It is at the heart of the trainings he provides to military and police forces the world over. Jack learned it from his own mentor, Professor Robert L. Humphrey (1923-1997), who first proposed it in his own books, *Values for a New Millennium* and *The Warrior Creed*.

The *Dual Life Value* is best summed up as a recognition of the sanctity of *all* life. This can become a central pillar to build upon in conflict resolution between warring parties. When you realize that the highest value for you *and* your enemy are the lives of your families, that you share commitment and devotion to your loved ones—even above yourself—you create a space of common ground that becomes the starting point for understanding and eventually peace. Humphrey, a veteran of World War II, saw this first hand in his travels throughout the world as a consultant for the US military, the State Department, and the CIA during the Cold War.

Deeply impacted by Humphrey's teaching, Jack Hoban would go on to become one of his most prolific disciples, integrating this approach to the combat and ethics trainings Jack provided to different branches of the military. Jack would go on to propose that the ultimate role of a warrior—who paradoxically, at times, must *take* life—is to first and foremost *protect life.* Through Jack's own scholarship of warriorhood, drawing on texts from ancient Japan to classical Greece, he found ample support for this interpretation . . . an interpretation that, in the context of modern, impersonal, mechanized armies, has been lost.

Jack Hoban trained soldiers to shift their self-concept from soldier-as-killer to that of a warrior-protector. To drive home this point, during lectures, Jack would project a giant picture of a grizzly bear lumbering along a river bank somewhere up in the Yukon and ask his trainees, "If you encountered this in the woods, would you be scared?"

"Sure."

"Of course," his students would say.

Then Jack would show the rest of the photo, revealing two grizzly cubs frolicking in the stream while they trailed after what was actually a mother grizzly.

"How many of you would be even more scared now?" Jack would ask.

Every hand would go up. Heads would nod. I would see people tugging at their collars. They would swallow or laugh uncomfortably. They'd realize Jack was on to something. It wasn't unusual for some to simply speak out, "Hell yeah," or, this being the Marines, "Fuck yeah."

Jack would then drive the point home: "The mother grizzly is more fearsome, not because she is a mindless killer, but because she is a protector, a *protector of life*. On some deep, archetypal level inside us, we know that this is the highest calling of anyone who is called into combat, mortal or otherwise. We know that facing someone or something protecting the lives that are precious to them is to face the most fearsome of opponents."

Jack goes on to explain that by embracing this ethos of protector of life, which is ultimately selfless and life affirming, the mere fighter, the conscripted soldier, the faceless nameless grunt, is transformed into a true warrior. Jack's is a framework, not just for the battlefield, but life in general.

The kicker, of course, is that Jack and his mentor, Robert Humphrey, would push their students one step further with the following concept of the Ethical Warrior:

An Ethical Warrior is a protector of life.
Whose Life?
Self and Others?
Which Others?
All Others, if possible.
Killing only when necessary to protect life.

All life includes even the enemy's life.

And that last bit was the revolution in thought Humphrey and Jack proposed.[21] To our modern conceptualizations of warriorhood that imagines a soldier going off to war to protect his or her loved ones—their ingroup or tribe—protecting even the enemy's life seems counterintuitive—a fatal weakness. After all, if we recognize that the enemy's life is sacred, like our own, aren't we setting ourselves up to choke at the crucial moment of confrontation?

But Humphrey and Jack, like Edward Tick, recognize that what is at stake in the life or death struggle of war is not just the life of a soldier, but their very soul, and the taking of life, even the enemy's, can have a shattering effect on it. This is especially true as we consider the cognitive dissonance of protecting the lives of our comrades while reading in the eyes of the enemy that he is simply doing the exact same thing—living up to his own ideal of loyalty to his brother and protection of his tribe, his ingroup. Many soldiers have written in personal accounts that, although they might not "like" the enemy soldier, they respect him and share a deep understanding of him, a recognition of a shared mission and misery.

It is here where we see the edges around our neat and tidy definitions of tribe, ingroup, whatever term we use to demarcate "us" from "them," begin to fray. For the soul recognizes a truth that the tribalism of politics would have us forget: that in the end there is only one tribe, and that is humanity. There is no us verses them. There is not "them" even, just "us," we humans, with lives of equal worth. No relative value, no tribal symbol, or ingroup membership can supersede that truth.

Tick reminds us that the soul, the psyche, the conscience, whatever term is you prefer, knows this. The soul does not recognize the imagined distinctions we create, socially and politically, to mobilize our young men and women to march off to war. After all, so many soldiers—my grandfather and Leo included—would testify that is was not abstract thoughts of patriotism or politics that kept them fighting in the trenches. Not even the thought of distant loved ones on the home front were as compelling in the urgency of battle as the loyalty to the buddy beside you. He, or she, is your brethren, in a way that no one could truly understand.

---

[21] This is truly less a revolution than a return to a more ancient and traditional ethic of the warrior.

No one could understand, except that enemy soldier, fighting opposite you.

Soldiers know this. So, when the heat of battle dies down and men and women must reflect on the lives they took, the lives they saw shattered left and right and ahead of them, their souls come under stress. In the tragic examples where, in retrospect, the justification of the fighting eventually is seen as less than noble—as many came to see the war in Viet Nam—this weight is even greater, and the psyche cracks beneath it.

But when the warrior can pass through the ethical paradox of battle and emerge with a sense that they have remained true to the ideal of warrior, of *protector of life,* the soul survives, not unscathed, but with fewer wounds. In Jack Hoban's trainings, he would stress that lethal force always had to be a final resort. He insisted upon this even in hand-to-hand combat situations when the fighting is so intense and the intimacy with your enemy is at its deepest and most profound. This is not always an easy choice. Actually, its honor and valor come from the fact that it is difficult. It requires monumental amounts of restraint, forbearance, discipline, and courage. But in the end, this choice preserves the warrior's sense of honor, their identity as protector rather than killer. Given a choice, we all would choose to be a protector rather than a killer or even executioner. In the end, choosing to *protect life* allows a soldier to maintain a hold of their own humanity.[22]

It's an admittedly high ideal but can produce stirring examples of courage on the battlefield, such as one Jack would share in his lessons. It took place during a firefight between soldiers loyal to the regime of Saddam Hussein and US Marines during the Iraq War. As the battle lines shifted throughout the course of fighting, a no man's land emerged between the forces: a pocket of battlefield wherein the wounded from both sides were trapped on the ground while crossfire from the opposing sides whirred overhead. Into this maelstrom of artillery and small arms, a single US Navy Corpsman dashed, braving enemy and friendly fire to retrieve his wounded comrades. He did so until he had recovered all the wounded American troops, carrying each on his shoulders to safety. This, for many, would have been an act of bravery and selflessness highly commendable in itself.

---

[22] It is worth noting that soldiers trained in this ethic, especially in the Marines, are believed to have lower rates of post-traumatic stress.

But it was what he did next that made his actions truly transcendent.

This Navy Corpsman, his ethic informed by the notion that all life is sacred, that in the final analysis even the enemy is our brother, that to preserve your humanity you must see the humanity of the other, even the man who was just shooting at you, this Corpsman went back into the no man's land to retrieve a wounded *Iraqi* soldier.

When he had carried the last of the wounded Iraqis to safety behind US lines where American medics tended to them—the medics also making no distinction between enemy and ally—the Corpsman collapsed behind the shelter of a berm to catch his breath. A Reuter's journalist embedded with the unit approached and asked him, "Why did you go and save Iraqis? They are your enemies."

The Marine, a young twenty-something, yet to finish college, having acted on an ethic he had internalized but could not articulate as eloquently as his instructors at Quantico had in the classroom said, panting, "That's what we do."

RECOLLECTIONS OF A GI
IX.
Robert Lewis Fowler

July 19th, Reserve

The next morning was July 19th, 1944. St. Lo was cleared and we were reverted to regimental reserve so that we could move around as long as we were in some type of cover. We had been forced to wait until after dark the night before to pick up the bodies of Tombrink and Micelli and carry them back to the medics. Tombrink was a big guy, and it was a job for four of us to carry him half a mile. This detail was organized by Jungle Jim, and he was one of the four carriers. He did not want to wait for the medics or Grave Registration people. This was a side of Jungle Jim we had not known until combat. Stateside, Captain Lassiter had been so "GI" and by the book, we had never seen any display of emotion or sentiment before.[23]

We were able to wash up and shave and we began receiving replacements. We received enough replacements that the First and Second Platoons were reformed as two separate platoons. This meant that I had to look at the six men I had left out of the forty-two I started with to decide which ones were sergeant material. I had Gill and Teply who were assistant squad leaders to begin with, so I made Gill platoon guide and Teply, Pennington, and Klentz my squad leaders.

---

[23] It is interesting to note that in Fowler's retelling of his story, this was the point when the name "Jungle Jim" first appears, as if Captain Lassiter's transformation from distant, cold commander to a warmer, more accessible human being took place in the crucible of combat and merited a whole new persona.

I tried to get Samson to give me Gordon Weeks. But no dice.

I was acting platoon leader and would have eventually received a battlefield commission, which I had really wanted. However, after the platoon was reorganized and we had a couple of days in which we were able to write letters and rest a little, I was called to Company Headquarters.

The First Platoon had been reorganized also, and Jake Sass had been assigned as platoon sergeant to replace John Cantoni, who had been wounded. In the meantime, my promotion to technical sergeant had gone through, and I had replaced Ryan officially. Jake Sass and I had reported to Jungle Jim, and we were introduced to two new second lieutenants fresh from OCS at Fort Benning. There went my battlefield commission, temporarily anyhow.

My new lieutenant was Stevens and Jake's was Gallagher. After introducing us, Jungle Jim then told the new officers that the sergeants will remain in command of their respective platoons until he told them differently. Lieutenant Greenlief had been assigned as company executive officer officially, and the next day he called us in to make our recommendations for decorations.

We made a gentleman's agreement that we would make our highest recommendation go to a deserving deceased member. We didn't think we had any Medal of Honor designees. I recommended Buster Brown for the Distinguished Service Cross, thinking he was KIA. His squad leader had reported him to me as a KIA, and I took his word for it. From all the reports I received and what I had observed, Buster deserved recognition, and because of the KIA report, we all agreed he was our best candidate. Because of so many heroic and unselfish acts performed by so many, we found it very difficult to pick one deed over another. Lieutenant Greenlief wrote me up for a Silver Star, but I thought I talked him out of it. However, it was changed to Bronze by higher headquarters. It was worth five points later, in a point system that was used to assign priority for those of us returning home after things were all over. This point system was unknown at the time, but in my case, it didn't matter one way or the other.

During this time in reserve I happened to see a French man walking up a road with a satchel over his shoulder. This satchel appeared to have some bottles in it. I assumed it was a beverage of some kind and negotiated with him for a bottle of unknown content. Neither one of us could speak the other's language, but the transaction was completed. The fact that my rifle was slung over my shoulder may have helped him understand me better.

Because we were in reserve, we could gather in small groups without drawing artillery fire, so I had a few guys help me sample my "purchase." I pulled the cork and passed the bottle to my left. The first man to sample it coughed and sputtered but was able to down a little and retain it with effort. The bottle proceeded around the group and was received in the same manner as the first. When it came back to me, I understood the reactions of the other guys. It was like straight alcohol and needed considerable "cutting." We later found out it was Colvados—180 proof, referred to as Buzz Bomb Juice. I gave the balance of the bottle to the first sergeant and never saw it again, nor the first sergeant for three days.

July 22nd

After about three days in reserve, I was told to get the platoon ready to move out. After receiving some replacements and reorganizing, I had about nineteen men, which meant I had thirteen new men and one new and inexperienced lieutenant—what we called a shavetail.

The Company minus the Third Platoon was moved over to the other side of St. Lo, and my platoon relieved a platoon of B Company in a position near an asylum. Our positions were dug around a large grotto with a field of fire to our south through an apple orchard. The wall of the asylum was ten feet high and extended straight away south from my left flank. All of this was on a steep hill with bombed out buildings in back of us, which were nothing more than rubble. The hill formed a cliff to our rear that could be scaled one person at a time. Just above this was a command post with boards across two stone rails about four feet high. We did have an EE8A telephone with a wire back to the First Platoon, which was just inside a long tunnel. They in turn were wired into Company Headquarters, which was up by the Cathedral de Notre Dame in St. Lo.

While there, we were able to work with Cannon Company Field Office and set up some prearranged barrages. The barrages were given code numbers for specific locations. We could call for barrage number G-7 and get fire on a specific crossroads, etc.

REFLECTIONS XII.
Warriors
Ted Neill

Steve Olson, my boss from the Center for Leadership and Ethics at Georgia State, claimed that the profound lesson of the battlefield, that recognition of not only *your* mortality but of the enemy's as well, created better leaders in government and civic life. This hard-earned knowledge fosters a greater understanding of the shared human condition and a deeper level of empathy for all others. Steve felt that the US had benefitted in the post-World War II years from the high numbers of leaders in government who were veterans. This gave us warrior elders who, as in traditional societies, carried this wisdom back from mortal combat. In ancient times, these warrior elders took the responsibility of de-escalating conflict and brokering peace within their tribes and with other communities, for they knew firsthand the face of war's suffering and its costs. Steve's theory was that this contributed to the spirit of bipartisanship and a level of civility in national and state government in the US that is all but gone in today's political discourse.

I read heartening signs of this warrior ethic in Grampa's memoir. It was not his fellow GIs who carried Grampa back to the safety of his own lines when he was shot, but rather surrendered *German* soldiers. At his memorial service in 2006, when my mother asked me to speak, it was that part of his story that I shared. My father did the same in Grampa's eulogy. Even at a time in my life when I had yet to meet Steve, Jack, or read the work of Edward Tick, it was this recognition of the humanity of these men that had hours before been his enemies that had stuck with me. When asked to sum up Grampa's life story in the briefest window, this was the illuminating anecdote both my father and I reached for.

Not included in Grampa's account was how, while waiting for help from the medics in the company of one particular German soldier, Grampa reached into his pocket and pulled out a picture of his daughter, my mother. Grampa spoke no German, and the German soldier spoke no English. But the surrendered German reached into his pocket to draw forth his own folded and crumpled picture. It was a picture of his own daughter, about the same age as my mother was at the time.

Of all the battles Grampa fought in life, I think this one was the most important—recognizing the human in his enemy, being able to switch from a mindset of combat to compassion, was what I believe preserved enough of his soul that, in time, he was able to find sobriety and even some peace in later life.

Post-battle, I could see how this recognition was still a crucial litmus test for honor and trust—turning former allies into enemies and enemies into allies. Those who could not make this shift remained enemies, their lives forfeit. I recognized it in Grampa's story of the American GI from the 320th Regiment that he and his buddy Al Grobe caught looting the bodies of his own fallen brothers. This GI, whom Grampa never names in his account, had chosen to enrich himself at the expense of his dead brethren. He did this while even neglecting his still living and injured GIs who needed help. This was a betrayal so great, a violation of an unwritten code, that execution seemed called for. It was telling to me that Grampa was persuaded by Al Grobe not to shoot the GI only by the idea that they could send him back up to the front lines in hopes he *would* get shot.

This redrawing of lines demarking enemy and ally, combat and compassion, was also evident in the fate of members of the SS. Grampa said these soldiers, even when captured, frequently would not cooperate. They would profess a steadfast belief in their Aryan superiority. They maintained a stance of opposition, and they would frequently try to escape or resist. When I asked Grampa how the US GIs dealt with the SS as they advanced and began capturing more German soldiers and officers, he shook his head, saying only, "They tended to be walked out into the woods and never made it back."

The gestures towards reconciliation that did take place in the aftermath of battle among Grampa and the Germans who did peaceably surrender, served me in my own interactions decades later. While on a trip in Ghana, I met a German girl who had grown up in the German Democratic Republic (GDR). This was the eastern side of the Berlin Wall that, throughout my childhood, had been under Soviet control. Upon meeting me, she was defensive and guarded saying, "I bet your grandparents tell stories about shooting Nazis."

"Not exactly," I said. "It was Germans who saved my Grampa, carrying him back to US lines when he was shot."

She and I are still friends to this day.

I suppose I look to these anecdotes as evidence of Grampa's own protector-of-life mentality. Like I said, I imagine this contributed to the healing that allowed him to string together a few good years that eventually added up to decades of sobriety. This was when I knew him. These were years when he was available to his daughters, his grandchildren. Grampa was even able to remain sober when his youngest son, Joe, died unexpectedly of a brain aneurysm, just days before his own son, Matthew (Grampa's youngest grandchild), was born.

Yet, I don't want to gloss over the wounds, physical, psychic, and spiritual, that Grampa and the men he served with suffered from. He told me how so many of them returned, only to experience night terrors and panic attacks. Many reported problems managing their drinking. They spoke of frequent drunkenness, blackouts, fighting with their wives, compulsive cheating, and even domestic abuse. Grampa and his surviving war buddies lost friends to suicide.[24] The demons of war had a deep hold on many of them. Edward Tick emphasizes that the services to support veterans are still woefully inadequate today and were even less supportive then.[25]

And thus, the chaos that my mother and her siblings grew up with. In the story of our family, one can even make a strong case for the intergenerational effects of poverty, abuse, and toxic stress— Grampa's emotional trauma transferred through experience and even epigenetics (in ways researchers are only beginning to understand) to his children and grandchildren. As I've mentioned, among the fourteen of us in my generation, around half of us struggle with mental health and substance abuse problems. This includes me. More than a handful of us have experienced institutionalization, homelessness, and/or incarceration.

Despite Grampa's slip when Evelyn died of cancer in 1991, he mainly retained his sobriety unbroken. In the lion's share of his later years he found some solace living, successfully, as the elder warrior.

---

[24] In *War and the Soul* as well as *Warrior's Return,* Tick writes that more American veterans die today from suicide than combat. That figure does not even include those who die from complications due to substance abuse.

[25] It may be surprising to civilians, but many veterans' organizations today, while providing valuable services and support to veterans and their families, only extend this support to post-9/11 vets. This does not include veterans of WWII, the Korean War, the war in Viet Nam, the Gulf War, or any of the smaller conflicts and tours of duties during those years.

He finally fused two of his lifelong loves together—driving[26] and serving his brothers and sisters of the military. On many days of the week he would shuttle vets in a large eighteen-seater van to doctor appointments all over the city of Omaha. These were men and women of WWII and other more recent ones. But they all were Grampa's brothers and sisters. He even donated blood at the VA every six to eight weeks, in hopes it could help other veterans undergoing surgeries.

For a man who was as taciturn and laconic as Grampa was, I have few pictures of him in which he is wearing an undiminished and unburdened grin. One is from before the war, when he was a young man, having found work, respect, and purpose in the National Guard, before he felt the need to posture and look older, before the clouds of loss gathered behind his eyes.

The other is decades later, standing next to that van, coffee cup in hand, and ready to go pick up other wounded warriors, ready for the prick of the phlebotomist's needle, still ready to bleed for anyone who needed it.

Grampa had found his place again, in service to others.

---

[26] I once joked with Grampa that the day he could no longer drive we'd have to take him back out behind the woodshed and shoot him—a plan he endorsed with a hearty laugh.

Photo: Robert L. Fowler 1995 with the VA van he would frequently volunteer to drive, bringing his love of driving and the National Guard together.

RECOLLECTIONS OF A GI
X.
Robert Lewis Fowler

July 23rd

One afternoon everything was pretty quiet until suddenly our BAR on the perimeter opened up. I jumped up and moved out to the position immediately, and my BAR man said that he had spotted a three-man Kraut patrol and opened up on them. They had ducked into an opening in the asylum wall and were protected from fire from the BAR. I ran over to the area where I had my reserve squad and tried to get them out of their holes. Pennington was the squad leader, and he was also trying, but all our men were new and scared. Despite our urging, they froze. My intention was to take them around in a flanking movement to see if we couldn't nail the Kraut patrol. But before I could get them moving, one of the Krauts had shot my BAR man and creased his right temple. The shooter then got away, back toward where they had come from.

Things quieted down, but now I had a wounded man to get back to the medics. With so many new soldiers, I didn't have a single man that was sure of finding his way back to where the First Platoon was. Our own new shavetail lieutenant locked up and couldn't speak. I decided to get the injured man back to the medics myself. When I returned to the line, Lieutenant Stevens thanked me for handling the situation. He confessed that he froze and didn't know what to do. I did tell him to stay with the platoon. During my absence, the three-man Kraut patrol tried our position once more. One of our guys managed to wound one, but the other two got away.

The Krauts sent two of their medics after their wounded man, and they picked him up and brought him into our position. The medics were wearing Red Cross arm bands, as did our medics, so my men didn't fire on them. They brought their own man in and rolled him into a shell hole and left him to die. I checked him. He was badly wounded and didn't have a chance. The German medics asked us to take them prisoner. One kept asking me, "Voo Chef?" I told him I wasn't any damn cook because I didn't know then that he was trying to speak to me in French because he already knew I didn't understand German. I mentioned earlier that we had removed our stripes, so without insignia of rank it was difficult for them to know who was who. My new men also had this trouble, but they eventually learned to recognize my bark. They did apologize later for freezing, but this was not unusual when men first got to the line.

July 25th

After three days on the line, a platoon from I Company came up to relieve us at night. I knew we were to return and join up with the rest of the Company near the cathedral at a certain time. I let Lieutenant Stevens show the relief lieutenant the different positions. They had been at Fort Benning together and had come overseas together. The mistake was letting them talk old times too long. My watch had rusted out from salt water at Omaha beach, so I wasn't sure of the exact time. It was tricky calling out a commanding officer, but I finally spoke up that we were late in meeting up with the rest of the Company and needed to move. Stevens cut short his reminiscing, and we moved out. The damage had been done, however. We reached the rendezvous at the cathedral late. I had never been chewed out like I was chewed out by Jungle Jim. He really let us have it from both barrels.

When we returned back to the reserve area, we were able to get a few hours of sleep. Then Greenlief called the platoon leaders in. We had to go back over our area where we had fought from July 15th. We were to plot the location of our dead on a map and also make positive identification. We were told to stick their bayonet in the ground with the rifle on it and the man's helmet on the butt of the rifle.

This was one of the most difficult duties we had up until then. These men had been out there for ten days. Due to mines in the area, the Grave Registration people were hesitant about going after bodies. I had to check dog tags or pay cards because flesh had fallen away from their faces, which made visual identification impossible. In most cases I knew where some of them had fallen, so I had some idea of whom I was looking at. One of them was Ralph McManaman, one of my squad leaders and also one of the guys we played football with in England. He was also one member of the group that had discussed our wound preferences.

When we returned from the body location task, we were given a chance to hop on a truck to the rear for showers. The quartermaster had set up a portable shower system. We entered one end and removed all our clothes. We saved our helmets, shoes, and canvas leggings. We then showered with GI soap. It was strong soap, and we needed it. In the beginning, we were short of drinking water but we could always find

large cider kegs. The Krauts always broke the
wine and cognac barrels as they retreated, but
they didn't bother with the cider, so we
usually filled our canteens with it. If a
person drank quite a bit of the cider it could
act as a laxative. One time during some heavy
shelling, fear overcame my ability to control
my bowels. I had to wear those pants until this
day when we went back to shower. We were issued
all clean clothing, and it felt really good. It
was also nice and quiet and peaceful, no
artillery—in fact no war back there. It was
tough to climb back on that truck.

When we returned back to the unit, we found out
the mail and tobacco rations had been brought
up. I cried while reading a letter from my
mother telling me not to take any chances and
get myself hurt. As I finished reading my mail,
Jungle Jim came by and he said: "Sergeant
Fowler, while you were gone the tobacco ration
came up, and I saved these for you." He handed
me two plugs of Horse Shoe chewing tobacco.
This was really appreciated and a surprise.

Back stateside, when we were out in the boonies
on tactical problems, it would be necessary for
Captain Lassiter to call a conference. Whenever
he would ask me a question, I would have to
spit before I answered him. Looking back, this
was part of my efforts to appear older. But I
could always see an annoyed expression on his
face when I had to spit. Yet here he was,
giving me two plugs of tobacco. He sure had
changed from the cold, unperturbable Captain
Lassiter to a very human person—Jungle Jim.
Later on, I found out it wasn't a change in his
basic personality as much as his manner of
acting out what he perceived a company
commander should be like.

The time that was spent at this location was used to re-equip ourselves with entrenching tools, grenade pouches, and other items we could attach to our cartridge belts. We also had received additional replacement troops, and we were able to pass on to them some of the tips we found useful.

It was during this period of time that Operation Cobra started. The Air Force must have gathered every heavy bomber in England for a daylight bombing mission of a tactical nature. Normally the big bombers like the B-17 and the B-24 were used for strategic targets, such as enemy aircraft plants and petroleum plants. In Operation Cobra, they were to saturate an area one mile wide and three miles long—three enemy lines—to "soften up" for Patton's Third Army to pour through and create the breakout from Normandy and to make the dash across France.

July 27th

A day or so later we pulled out of the assembly area and moved back through St. Lo to the south edge of town, near where I had my platoon a few days before. My platoon was to remain at a point known as the LD (line of departure) and the time of departure was 3:00 PM. We arrived at the LD about an hour early, so I spread out my men of the Second Platoon and told them to relax and wait for the order to move out.

The Third Platoon's LD was in the exact area that my platoon position had been a few days before. It was difficult to get up to it unless you knew the exact route. My buddy, Leo Samson, and his platoon leader, Lieutenant John Campbell, asked me to guide them up there. I told Lieutenant Stevens to stay put and that I would be back in a few minutes and also what I was going to do.

When I returned from guiding the Third Platoon into position, I was just in time to see the last of my platoon moving out. It was also just in time to meet Captain Lassiter and hear him ask why my platoon was jumping off from the LD ahead of time. I told him where I had had been, and he said to get up to the front of the platoon and tell Lieutenant Stevens to get back to the tail end of the platoon and stay there.

I was able to get the platoon back to the LD without incident, and we waited for 3:00 PM. At that time, all platoons moved out. At the far edge of town, we had to move through a German mine field. These were Teller mines, which were meant for anti-tank use. It takes 250 pounds of pressure to detonate these mines, so we were able to move through carefully. It was all done without enemy fire of any kind. We expected to get fired upon when we left the edge of town and started to move across open fields. We were very vulnerable targets. Regardless, we were to proceed south out of St. Lo for a couple of miles. Then we were to pivot and move east toward the town of Vire.

We reached a chateau at the point where we were to turn. L Company, being the left unit, had to stay in place and let I Company on the right make the wide part of the turn. It was during this operation that the enemy opened up. I was with my right squad, since they were the link of contact with I Company. We moved out across an open field and closed in around the chateau and the outbuildings. We discovered twenty-one enemy troops in a barn, and we hadn't received hardly any enemy fire of any kind.

We consolidated our position, which allowed I Company to complete their turning movement. They were beginning to get some resistance but were still pushing forward.

I had my platoon up along a hedgerow and was waiting for word to move out when we began getting mortar fire. I knew the best way to react was to move forward, so I told the platoon to move out up to the next hedgerow. But still with so many new troops, I didn't get much results, so I said, "Follow me," and I climbed over the hedgerow and took off across an open field to the next hedgerow, which was only about 100 yards. I looked back and not one of my men had followed.

I moved on up to another hedgerow, and everything was quiet. I could hear someone's clothing scratching against stubble, and it seemed to be coming from the other side of the hedgerow. I carefully looked over the hedgerow through some foliage, and there was a Kraut starting to run down a road. I couldn't get my rifle lined on him very quickly because of the brush, but when I fired, he increased his pace.

After I fired, an enemy machine gun opened up across the road. About that time, Lieutenant John Campbell and his runner showed up from the Third Platoon, so we were able to toss a few grenades across the road. Since the target was only about 30 yards away, we would let the safety handle of the grenade flop over after pulling the pin, then count "one," "two," and heave it. It took four and a half seconds from the time the safety handle released the striker, which started the fuse, to detonation. If you delayed throwing just right, the grenade would explode in the air and scatter the shrapnel better. This also gave the enemy less time to react if they saw the grenade coming. The tactic worked. The machine gun fire stopped, and we felt a little more secure in our position.

I told Lieutenant Campbell where my platoon was and said I was going back to bring them up. I had just gotten up on my feet when I felt a blow in my upper left thigh. I knew I was hit. I took a dive back to the ground and rolled over a couple of times. This was in grass about a foot high. If it was a sniper, I hoped this would confuse him some. I moved my left leg to see if it was usable. I had full control of it, but it was extremely painful to move it in certain directions. The point of entry was about four inches below my left hip bone, and it felt as though the bullet was in my scrotum. That was where the worst of the pain was, and I wondered if the bullet had passed through my thigh to hit me there.

I had visions of lying in the grass and being captured or bleeding to death. Even though the bleeding was not bad, my imagination presented a lot of possibilities. I told Campbell I was hit but I would go back and tell Captain Lassiter to get some help up to Campbell's position.

I jumped up and started back to where the platoon was. I found out that fear and shock can overcome a lot of pain. I located Captain Lassiter and told him where Campbell was and that I was hit. Also, I told him where my platoon was and recommended Chester Gill to take my place.

My next concern was getting to the aid station back from the front line. We always knew it would be only a few hundred yards to our rear, which it was. One of the sergeants from the weapons platoon came over to me with two German prisoners. The sergeant was wounded in the back by shrapnel but still able to function. He made the Germans get on either side of me to help me get to the aid station.

The aid station was in a house in St. Lo that wasn't too badly damaged. I was given a morphine shot and also penicillin. I remained on a stretcher for quite some time, until a trail was cleared through the rubble of the town. They placed our stretchers crossways on jeeps, which were able to get back through St. Lo to a road where we were taken by ambulance to the field hospital.

At the hospital, I was undressed down to my skivvies, shoes, and helmet. I immediately went to sleep from the morphine and was awakened by the feeling that I was being carried and opened my eyes to find I was on a stretcher with two more German soldiers on either end of it. They were also prisoners being put to work.

I was x-rayed, but the original x-ray was not positioned correctly to detect the bullet. The medic initially thought I might have been faking the injury to get off the line. I suggested he take the x-ray again, lower this time. After that, he was able to determine where the bullet had lodged. It had ricocheted and lodged in my left ischium, resting near the femoral artery and a nerve that had caused the pain to radiate to my groin.[27] As a result, I

---

[27] My grandfather told me once that one of the things that had occurred to him when he was initially hit by the ricocheted bullet was that he was thankful that he had at least one child by that point in his life—my mother, Kathleen—because, due to the way the pain was radiating from his leg to his groin, he feared the worst and that he would not be able to have any more children. However, by the end of his life, he and his wife Evelyn had raised five girls and three boys who have gone on to

enjoyed my first airplane ride on a C47 hospital plane across the channel to a hospital near Wrexham, North Wales.

November 1944 – July 27, 1945

Four months later I was sent back to France to a replacement depot near the town of Noyon for limited duty as an instructor of infantry tactics. The bullet had moved slightly away from the nerve, and I experienced no further pain, even though it is still in there to this day.

I was lucky enough to have enough points to be on the first wave returned stateside, and I had the pleasure of seeing Lady Liberty in New York Harbor on July 27, 1945. After a couple of years, I rejoined the National Guard, still the 134th Infantry, and received my commission as a second lieutenant. Eighteen years later I retired as a major. I still feel respectful when I salute the flag.

---

have fourteen grandchildren—all of whom were able to meet their grandfather.

REFLECTIONS XIII.
Finding St. Lo
Ted Neill

It was the damn twenty-one-gun salute at my grandfather's funeral that broke my resolve and left me in tears.

I had made it through the length of the funeral mass that morning with a sort of flat determination. This allowed me to go through the motions of the service: the three readings, a sermon, followed by the consecration of the host, communion, then dismissal. Raised in the Catholic church, I could follow the well-worn paths mechanically. The familiarity was comforting.

But as Grampa's ashes were carried down the aisle, the reassuring sequence of ritual was shattered by the crack of three rifles. Three service members fired their guns into the sky while a fourth called out the prompts: Ready. Aim. Fire. Ready. Aim. Fire.

They were old men themselves, their dress regalia from different services and different wars, but their faces were uniform with solemnity. They cracked off seven simultaneous rounds, quick and precise. Their lifelong skills polished from the many recent funerals of their contemporaries.

It was that unexpected eruption of gun fire that broke through the shell I had enclosed my own feelings in. Before I could follow the rest of the mourners and family outside, I turned around, sat back down in the pew, and wept.

The echoes of the gunfire faded and were replaced by the rising, steady hum of respectful conversation—growing murmurs from the foyer as the mood of the funeral receded and the regular rhythms of life reestablished themselves—allowing us all to continue, blissfully forgetting that the hourglass is running for all of us.

At least until the next death reminds us that we're all on borrowed time.

After what felt like a few minutes, I looked up to see I was all alone in the nave. Everyone had left. Everyone except for my cousin David. David, who is in so many ways my opposite—fair and blond, tall, athletically gifted, politically conservative. David, who always displayed a typically midwestern reserve more like Grampa than me. He had remained seated alone in the pews. The shock of the guns had pierced something in Dave too. Neither of us could even make eye contact in that moment, but I felt a profound gratefulness for him, a sense of solidarity in loss and grieving that words or a look could never convey. His quiet presence alone was enough.

Just like Grampa.

That solidarity was shattered later at my aunt Mary Anne's home where a number of us gathered for a meal. While I sat with David, his sister Kathleen, and my aunt Elyse reminiscing about Grampa around the fireplace, David's mother Margie erupted in the kitchen. She was shouting out in rage that Mary Anne would chose *that* afternoon to share stories and complain about Grampa's out-of-control drinking. His drinking had left deep scars on Mary Anne's life, however, and she felt she had a right. Margie had been hurt too, but she felt dwelling on it was disrespectful to the father they had just buried and mourned.

"There was more to him than that," Margie said.

I don't even remember the particulars of the other accusations and curse words hurled back and forth. I never even caught sight of the two sisters fighting, only heard them as their voices grew louder and more distraught. David, Kathleen, their partners, and I broke for the door, walked to our cars, and left.

The brief funeral-day armistice between the five remaining daughters and one son (Bob Jr.) of Robert and Evelyn Fowler, the only surviving children, siblings who found themselves feuding even into adulthood, had dissolved. It was a sad intrusion of the truth we all had suppressed in the illusion of harmony that funerals make. That truth was this: the fighting, the fractured family dynamics, the legacy of hurts and disappointments from Robert Lewis Fowler would continue long after his death.

As families and generations go, that has always been a truism, I am afraid. Family cycles, family dynamics—good and bad—are eternal. Inevitable as they are, as our own human failings and shortcomings. And perhaps, to bring this story of Robert Lewis Fowler to some high-gloss, Hollywood resolution would feel inauthentic. I think it would even feel incomplete and dishonest in light of the man we knew.

But just as family dysfunction feels eternal and inevitable, timeless even, I am aware there are other things so cyclical in time that they seem to transcend it. The rise, fall, redemption, and *fall again* of our heroes, for one. The love-hate, reverence-resentment, seeking-rejecting relationships we have with the generations before us. History has a way of reminding us of this constant churn and burn of human stories. The names and actors change, but the stories and themes remain, becoming familiar, so much so that we recognize the archetypes rising with their own anonymous brilliance out of the dust and wreckage of what were once distinct individuals and personal stories.

When I think of those things that are eternal, I also am reminded of those moments in my own life, those peak experiences, those transcendent moments we all share. Points when we transcend the flow of time around us and experience brief contact with something more eternal, moments when we feel distant from the daily grind of the world yet intimate with the rest of the universe itself.

I've had those moments: receiving a kiss on the lips while leaning against the wall of a gym, having given a girl starring in a high school play flowers; climbing to the top of a hill in the Highlands of Scotland where stars hang alongside me while a wind blows in from the North Sea with such force that I have to grip the stone with white knuckles to remain in place; standing under a shelter, listening to thunder and watching raindrops streak through the light of a flickering streetlamp on a balcony in Nairobi.

Or sitting on a hill in the prairie with Grampa, just outside Fort Robinson, one of the stops on our trip across Nebraska together. The Lincoln Town Car parked on a roadside, close to a privately owned herd of bison. The fourteen-hundred-pound animals grazing peacefully while the two of us sit side by side, listening to the music of our youth: Glenn Miller's band playing *In the Mood* in Grampa's case, U2's *Joshua Tree* album in mine. Otherwise, we sit in silence, watching the sun, the color of a flame without smoke, set in a clear sky, the tips of the grass shaking in the wind.

Photo: Bison grazing near Fort Robinson, Nebraska.

I knew Grampa was a man of many moments like these. In those years of sobriety, when he had a reprieve from the demons of his past and the ghosts that stalked his memories, I would catch him sitting on his back deck, watching the play of light in the cottonwoods of his backyard as the sun rose in the mornings. He was a man to whom the beauty of the natural world was never lost. He was drawn to it and had no shame in showing it. I see it in those moments in his story—when he is an eighteen-year-old farm boy peeking around the window sash of a train car to catch a glimpse of the moon over the snowfields of Donner pass; when he is surprised by the flash of a flying fish as it careened over the sparkling waters of the Pacific while he rode a water taxi out to Catalina island; when he saw the Emerald Isle, the land of his own ancestors, for the first time from the deck of a steamboat and felt the breath go out of his chest; or playing football in the slanting summer sunlight on the moors of Cornwall.

When I consider those moments, I still feel close to him. These were intervals in his own life when he was transported to a place of belonging, of oneness. Maybe he felt whole. I believe he fought for those moments of peace and transcendence as much as he fought for the men at his side. Not to protect it, as we can't protect transcendence; by its very nature it doesn't need us to. It was beyond him, beyond all of us, to do that. But I imagine that Grampa fought in the hopes that, after the bullets stopped flying, after he did his duty, he might return to those spaces, where peace is eternal, where the prairie wind is still blowing.

I hope he is there now.

What have I learned at the end of all this? That perfection is a standard that is too high to hold our heroes up to, for any generation, much less ourselves? Certainly. Even after reflecting on our time together, reviewing his memoirs in detail, it remains hard to guess, for me, what sort of role model Grampa would be today. I don't know where he might stand on the crises facing our nation now, resurgent racism, sexism, homophobia, environmental degradation, climate change, a rise in xenophobic nativism masquerading as patriotism, police violence and the mass incarceration of people of color, and a national government that is by turns corrupt, gridlocked, and authoritarian, with shades of fascism.

Then what *have* I learned? That Grampa was a war hero? That he was flawed human being?

I knew both those things already.

What stands out to me at the end of this, actually, is how closely those two things sit next to each other in the narrative that is Grampa's life. The triumphs and tragedies, intertwined as intimately as lovers, partners like Bob and Evelyn, who coexist together despite the mounting history of hurts and betrayals that accrue over the years. For the vines and creepers that connect us go deep; the ones that heal and the ones that hurt become indistinguishable from one another. This is especially true in Grampa's case. As I consider those days in Normandy to those days on a hill outside St. Lo and then the years that followed, I see, paradoxically, that the very thing that gave Grampa's life purpose, that brought valor to his story, was the same thing that broke him. It's true for him and so many of the men who served and died alongside him. It's a twin blessing and curse that we are lucky if we are able to avoid ourselves.

Did I find the broader lessons from Grampa's "greatest" of generations, some key to build fortitude as we ride out the chaotic national and global landscape of today? Not really. Only some solace that, indeed, things have always been chaotic. Stability is the exception. Change the rule.

It is also impossible to read Grampa's story and reflect on his family without growing aware of the poignant truth: that the conflicts and movements painted in broad strokes by history have profound and lasting impact on the lives of individuals. These impacts get lost due to their sheer, overwhelming number and idiosyncratic nature. They have a granular quality that only comes through in the narrow, limited memoirs of individuals. This is in contrast to the thick history books, which pull back so far to offer us scope that the individual soldier and his unique suffering becomes another number on a morning-after-action report, a tally in a column, a faceless name incised into the stone of a memorial.

Is there some metaphor to draw between Grampa's broken nature, the contrast between his valor and his venality, that provides some key insight into the character of our nation? Are his cycles from saint to sinner, light to shadow, a reflection of our own? The angel and devil on either of his shoulders the same opposing voices of virtue and vice that have alternatively steered the course of our nation?

Or could that just be me reaching too far, trying to force a tidy ending that I promised not to, a glossy resolution that, in the fullness of time, isn't really there? Who knows what our country will be in the light of history, after so many of cycles from heroes to villains, liberators to oppressors, from city on a hill to pit of corruption? It's impossible to see from here to which side the scales will fall.

But we know, in time, they will.

I don't feel guilt for speculating. There is no shame in wondering, in trying to make meaning out of meaninglessness. As Edward Tick would remind us, it is what we humans have always done—yearn for meaning, impose order, seek out narrative structure in the mess of our lives, a structure that will offer some purpose for it all. Yet despite the long view of deep time, one thing I am aware of is that when considering our decisions in the present and the immediate future, our choices now *do matter*. A reflection on the lives of my aunts and uncles and my cousins in the wake of Grampa's life confirms that truth for me. So, we should do our best to make the right choice. Otherwise, future generations might find us wanting. Will our legacy be one of pain and loss, or love and healing? In each moment, the decisions we take, the choices we make, tip those scales in one direction or another.

And if there is one thing I have learned from being curator of sorts of all these stories, it is this: the coming generations, those younger than we, they are already watching, waiting, and judging, as they will bear the burden of the choices in our present.

PART II

Gordon Edward Cross: Diary of a Front Line Medic

REFLECTIONS XIV.
Gordon Edward Cross
Ted Neill

While researching the history of the 35th Division and the 134th Regiment on the website maintained by former members and their families, among PDFs of after-action reports, declassified intelligence briefs, and personnel rosters, I happened upon a personal diary titled "The Diary of a Front Line Medic — WWII" by Gordon Edward Cross. Amid the reports and unit histories, written in a dry, objective tone that I had already come across, Cross's account stood out for its personal nature.

Once I had begun reading, I couldn't stop, finishing it in one long sitting.

The diary had been generously posted and shared on the 134th Regiment's website by Gordon Cross's son, William (Bill) Cross as an attempt to ensure that his father's experience and his story were not "lost to history."

I reached out immediately, somehow knowing that Cross's story had to be shared alongside my grandfather's own. There was a breathless quality to it that made it riveting. This is reinforced by the urgent present tense Cross wrote in. This as-it-is-happening quality denies us, the readers, any reassurance that the author of these missives, written *in situ,* even survived. These are no post-fact reflections written in the comfortable distance of the past tense. Gordon's writing put me in Normandy and onward into the depths of wartime Europe in a way even my grandfather's account had not. The extraordinary fact that Cross survived, without serious injury, even to the end of the campaign, provided follow-through to the story of the 134th that my grandfather, evacuated after being shot outside St. Lo, could not. The fact that he had served alongside my grandfather, in the very same regiment provide me a further window into what Grampa had experienced. The notion that there is a possibility that Gordon had even been one of the medics who may have tended to Robert L. Fowler when he had been shot, sends chills across my skin.

Cross's eye for detail, his lyrical style, and a temperament that differed in the extreme from my terse grandfather. Gordon's words helped me to see, hear, smell, touch, and taste the harrowing hellscape of the battlefield in a way I never had before. Cross's account is visceral; all the more powerful for its brevity, written almost like a poem, the staccato beat of scene after scene, one close call after another, one glimpse of death followed by another, even more grisly. It compelled me forward to reach the end. Cross's account is fighting and writing at its fiercest. It possesses the searing brilliance of a flare that you can't look away from, even as it burns your retinas and turns your eyes to water.

But I read for an even deeper reason. After hearing my grandfather's stories, knowing and working alongside active duty military and retired veterans, I've lived a long time with the knowledge that I don't have what it takes to be a combat soldier on the front lines. While I have worked in warzones in Northern Uganda and Afghanistan, and I've witnessed the bloody casualties of street violence in Accra, Ghana, and Nairobi, Kenya, I've been spared the ordeal of real combat. As I mentioned in the first sections of this book, I know my own disposition and temperament are too sensitive, too fragile for the soul-crushing horrors and the heartrending choices of battle. Hence my own career path that steered me into roles and careers of caregiving: as a hospice assistant in an orphanage for children with HIV/AIDS; as a teacher in that same orphanage; and eventually as a professional in the public health field. In addition to that, beneath it all has been the firm sense that my first identity is that of a writer, an artist.

Not exactly the steel-jawed soldier with a steady hand or a flinty glare.

So it was in Gordon Edward Cross, a medic who had reassured his family that he would be safe while he served from the safety of the X-ray unit, a man who preferred a career performing as a singer or working as a photographer, that I identified with. Even in Gordon's compulsion to write his story down on scraps of paper stuffed into his helmet, I could see myself. I had done the same thing as a way of processing my own traumas in Africa, scribbling in a journal each night under a mosquito net by the light of a candle after another child had died. It was an impulse to impose structure, pattern, meaning on the chaos around us, lest we be overwhelmed by that rising wave of nihilism that the destruction of lives, adults or children, brought to bear on us. A wave that threatened to snuff out any hope or purpose, much less faith in anything good.

In Robert Lewis Fowler I had a grandfather, a linear blood relative, in whom I could see a man with my build, my lean stature, even my hair. In him, I could see my *physical* self.

But Gordon Edward Cross, in the medic-photographer-turned-writer, I could see something more. In Gordon, I heard the voice of an artist, a healer, and my own *spiritual* kin. I could see myself in his place. In his reactions, I could imagine my own. And I could only hope that, in similar circumstances, I could rise to the occasion as he did.

I am deeply grateful that his son Bill shared his story with us.

Introduction
By William G. Cross

Like many combat veterans, Dad never talked much about it. Oh, he'd say a few things now and then, but I was too young to understand or appreciate what he went through and didn't have the foresight to follow up and have any detailed discussions about his experiences. My mother said that, also like many veterans, he suffered from nightmares years after his return from the war. Dad never thought he'd be drafted, let alone see combat. Once there, he never thought he'd be coming home. Entering the army at age thirty-eight and trained as an X-ray technician, he felt secure in the knowledge that he'd be attached to some sort of field hospital far from the front. Such was not to be the case.

In 1944, with the war raging in France, there was a constant need for replacements. At the time, anyone with any sort of medical training often got sent right to the front. So it was he found himself in a foxhole one night with a young soldier who was wishing he were ten years older. Dad inquired why. The young man said he was twenty years old but had heard that those who were thirty or older were never sent to the front. Dad at the time was thirty-nine. He said he didn't have the heart to tell the young man.

Drafted in October 1943, Dad became a member of the 35th Infantry Division, a unit that attacked thirty-five out of its first forty-five days in combat. It was a group that suffered over 23,000 causalities during WWII, a level which represents a 180 percent attrition rate. Originated during the Indian Wars, the men of the 35th wore the Santa Fe shoulder patch, a white cross on a blue field honoring the men who blazed the Old Santa Fe Trail. Although he was never seriously wounded, he saw many that were.

This diary is edited only for grammatical style and was compiled by my father after the war from bits of paper he carried with him throughout the war in his pack or helmet headband. It represents his words regarding what he experienced as a frontline medic assigned to the 134th Infantry Regiment Medical Detachment between July 1944, and May 1945, from Omaha Beach to the fall of Germany.

Diary of a Front Line Medic — WWII
Gordon Edward Cross
35th Division — 134th Infantry Regiment

Florence, my wife, seven months pregnant, was expecting me home for dinner, but suddenly I couldn't leave Upton, New York, and even telephone calls were forbidden. When I didn't call, Florence knew I wouldn't be home for dinner for a long time.

Our ship, the Dominion Monarch, left New York May 1, 1944. Crossing the Hudson River on the ferry, I could see our London Terrace apartment building. We marched on board to the strains of "Strip Pokka," played by a WAC band. Jammed into the mess hall, still wearing ODs with a full horseshoe roll, we were like sardines and hot as hell. Finally, hammocks were slung head to toe, as close as possible. During the day they were rolled and stacked, and I never saw mine again after the first night. The food was poor and some guys didn't eat half the meals. One fellow I knew lived on candy bars.

The fourteen-day voyage was not bad. We had good weather. Two or three times there were alerts and sub chasers dropped ash cans around the ship. We gathered we were on a northerly route in a convoy of about fifty vessels. I met Creighton, Brickey, and Dugan. Arrived in Liverpool Sunday, May 14, and disembarked to a recording of my old friend Frank Parker singing "Begin the Beguine."

Loaded onto a tiny train, we traveled to Warminster where we arrived about 11:00 PM. Black as pitch. There had been an air raid the night before. We lined up and stumbled about six miles, carrying that heavy pack. It was so dark, I tied a white handkerchief to the man ahead.

The camp was called "Chalcutor" – "Chocolate". It was a tent city, set up that day on the summer place of the sister-in-law of the Duke of Kent. We were handed two blankets and a brand-new army cot, which we struggled to set up with numb fingers by match light. This was May, but I have never been colder. It was a penetrating dampness that chilled to the bone.

The next morning at daybreak we were all out scavenging for paper, hay, anything for insulation. At night we went to bed early and piled all our equipment on top of us to keep warm. Got to talking to a tent-mate from Connecticut named George Comer. He knew my good friend and fellow singer, J. Alden Edkins. In fact, Alden was now working on George's uncle's farm in East Haddam, Connecticut. (George was destined to become my good friend.)

The English countryside was lovely. I heard my first cuckoo. Beautiful flowers in the little villages, but cadence marching on the paved roads was "for the birds." With luck, I managed to get on as "mail clerk," which got me out of the hikes and KP details. My buddy, Comer, was having real trouble with the hikes, so I managed to get him on the mail detail too. He was most grateful.

The small English towns were very attractive in a quaint way, but the shops had nothing much to sell but postcards. Tried English ale and stout. Decided English tea's better than their coffee. Most people very poor by our standards. If a man drove a car, he couldn't afford tobacco.

We were assigned to a "replacement" package. Theoretically, this included the replacements needed by a division in combat. Men began leaving, a few at a time, depending on their specialty numbers. Finally, our package was alerted and moved about 20 miles to "Tilshed," a forsaken wind-swept camp which became more pleasant with warmer weather. Creighton, Deeds, and I put on several shows which the boys seemed to enjoy. Deeds did a "fire-eating" act, played the accordion, and accompanied me on some old "chestnuts." Our GI show was a big hit.

Spent the early morning hours of "D-Day" hanging over fences in the woods and lined up before the latrines, which were hopelessly overworked. Overhead we heard the roar of the planes and sometimes could make out the black and white stripes on the wings. The big attack was on.

Moved to a staging area about 6:00 PM, July 12th. This was it, and we were a bit grim. We'd had inspections all the way along, but here we got final shortages, put on wool ODs with gas-impregnated fatigues over them. Next morning, we moved out to nearby Weymouth, where we could see ships waiting in the harbor. Weymouth seemed nice, and I thought I'd like to arrive under different circumstances.

All along I felt fortunate. I was an X-ray technician headed for an evacuation hospital, while a lot of these guys were headed for the front lines.

Crossed the channel at night. Picked up the French coast early in the morning. About noon we reached Omaha Beach, where there was tremendous activity. Boats taking men in, ducks unloading supplies, sunken ships, burned-out tanks, barrage balloons—all the grim evidence of war. Went to shore in a small boat. A man just back of me killed himself and the bullet wounded an officer behind him. On shore, still carrying that huge horseshoe pack, we walked up a long landing platform, along a rough sandy beach to a road running parallel to the beach.

Waited for our group to assemble and then began to walk. They said it was a couple miles. We walked three, and then they said two miles. Tapes along the track road read "cleared of mines to ditch." We walked miles, but it was still two more—now one mile, now 300 yards—just another mile. Finally we made it. It was an empty field. We'd passed through a couple small French villages, where old men and women passed out cider—made us feel like the conquering heroes—no mistaking the gratitude of these people. I've never been more tired. I spread out a raincoat and slept.

Next morning, we took off in trucks. Now we began to see what war was really like. Isigny was one town; "was" is right. I never dreamed of such destruction. Piles of rubbish, half houses, which were even worse. Trees stripped of leaves look obscene—fields churned. Here were hundreds of veterans going back to the front and also a lot of CEs That means "combat exhaustion." Where is that evacuation hospital? "No, your spec. number won't be changed." They seem to need a lot of medics.

All the combat men have 29th or 35th Division patches. The 29th came in on D-Day. I heard a couple of vets talking—"Sam got it, and so did Ed and Pete and that officer and the staff sergeant. There are about four left out of the whole squad."

How lucky I am to be in X-ray! Strange they should need so many X-ray technicians way up here! Several of the medics are in X-ray.

Air raid—pretty red balls floating through the air. "Keep that helmet on! That is lead and steel floating around up there!"

Sound asleep—clang, clang—a gas attack! Dear God, where is that mask. . . . There, I've got it! You clumsy bastard. How about my hands? Should I try to get into that impregnated clothing? Yelling and screaming from the CE's. Good lord, they don't have gas masks! What's that sound? The all clear? Thank God!

"Cross, Dugan!!!" Well, here we go. It's the 35th Division. What's that about spec. numbers? Mine is Medical Technician. What the Hell is that? Not litter bearer, thank heaven.

Our truck stops at the 134th Regiment Service Company. "You'd better dig in good—there are some holes. There was a raid two nights ago. See that truck and those shrapnel holes?" A guy tries to tell us that it isn't too awfully bad. He's a might doleful Joe, but I guess he means well. I wish he didn't look so sad.

Next morning, we move up to Regimental Headquarters—a small tent in a field. "Meet Sgt. Ozzie and Major"—the major seems like a nice guy. "You're from New York and a singer? Well, glad to have you." This guy seems smooth—he will fix me up, I know.

We watch a 1,000-plane strike at St. Lo. It is wonderful, though we didn't realize how wonderful. Blasovich and Winters go to Second, Casey to First, Dugan and Cross to Third Battalion.

Dead cows, swollen horses—stink, trees smashed, fields pockmarked. Along a wooded road into a grove where there is a tent, a jeep, several bicycles, and half a dozen men. There is gunfire close by. "How far is the front?" All around there—a half circle ahead. Why aren't these guys afraid? Some of them are! That guy has a haunted look in his eyes, another is trembling, and, dear God, he is crying! Captain Matt, battalion surgeon and our commanding officer, has a worried look too. "Well, paint Red Crosses on your helmets." Now I know there is no X-ray tent. I felt sorry for Dugan, coming up when he said to Sgt. Osborne that it was a shame to spend all that time and money to train a man for X-ray and then . . .

Third Battalion is in two sections. Dugan and I go to Captain Friedman's section. He seems like a cool duck. Several of the guys seem nice, but a couple are very nervous. "You'd better dig in well, some shelling here." Dugan and I pick out a spot and dig. Whistle, crack, we hit the dirt. Crack again. Those are 88s and nobody needs to tell us. Dig, dig, deeper, deeper. Now a roof, more screaming shells. Dugan and I scramble down and lie trembling. My knees won't stop shaking. That must be all for now. "Where did those hit?" One in the road, one across above us, and one lower.

Wounded coming in. I do what I can. Unfold litters, etc. How those guys rip into that clothing. Scissors slither up a pant leg, rip off a shirt sleeve. "Sulfa powder, carlyles, what in hell are carlyles?" Oh, those paper-covered bandages with the tails on them. Triangles for slings, leg splints, plasma, morphine syrettes.

"Bob, Cherry, Cross, Jack, litter squad to the CP" Grab a litter blanket somebody, got an aid kit? By jeep for about a mile—that's St. Lo. From here on foot. Keep moving! Hit the dirt! Let's go—that building is the CP.

"This fellow will guide you up." "Yah, it's my buddy, this way." Up through utter desolation. Your mind refuses to believe such destruction. No building not hit. Dead bodies. Through littered streets, into a church, down the front steps. The soldier tells us, "He's in the middle of that field over there, about 200 yards. I can't go any further because we're under observation from here."

"Well, if they can see us let's stand up so they can tell we're litter bearers. That's our only chance." Nothing happens. We go on over a wall, across piles of rubble. How will we ever get a patient back up this way on a litter? Now we're in the field, must be further. There he is. Bandages, morphine. Let's go. R. R. R. ratatat, we hit the dirt! That's a burp gun! Anybody hit? Christ, we can't stay here! Grab hold and swing right, away from that gun. Let's go! My lungs are bursting. Set him down a minute. Change hands. Let's go. Up over the wall. There's the church, here's his buddy. "What in the world were you two guys doing out there?" "We're from the Navy, we were just looking for some excitement."

Same litter squad to the CP, now set up in a cement crypt in the St. Lo cemetery. Casualties in outpost up ahead, but because of observation can't go forward until dark. Now 3:00 PM. Climb into a hole in the graveyard, protected by a big headstone. Whistle, crunch! Are you all right? Kicked dirt all over us. More shelling. Thank Heaven for a good deep hole. Tombstones over the living. Scream, crunch, that one hit a stone close by. It's getting dark. "Hey, you guys, let's go!" One man is missing, but we can't wait. Up this street, turn down to the left, over the fence, cross the street, through the gate. "Quiet, watch the light!" Down the stairs into a basement lit by a couple candles. Mattresses along one side. Several guys are hit, and there are only two of us. Well, we'll carry the worst one and lead the walking wounded. Broken leg. My God, he's over six feet. We can't even get him up those steps, but we do. Now back to the CP. Left here, now right, over that fence, across the field. "Down, damn it, they're shelling the road." Run, for God's sake, we can't stay here. "Wait, I can't hold on any longer." Rest a minute. Another 100 yards. Down again. "Sorry, but I can't do any better." Let's go again. "Wait, I gotta stop." A mile and a half of this, it can't be much further. Here's the jeep, thank God. I've never been so tired in my life.

We are going to move up. We pack supplies into packs and move up to that same St. Lo cemetery and dig in. A shell hits a mausoleum we'd inspected two minutes ago. Now I dig in earnest. What are these bones? I'm a ghoul! Sorry, but the dead must make way for the living. Better one alive than two piles of bones. We continue digging among the graves.

We move on into town. That's a laugh. There isn't a whole house standing. We "captured" a bunch of bicycles, so here I am riding and pushing a bike through St. Lo. Dead men, some GIs. Caved-in earthen sacks. Were these once living men? Bloated, turning black. The smell of death is everywhere. On single file through the rubble. Watch out for booby traps! There's one taped off by the engineers, a Heinie pistol. An underground hospital, they say it was trapped with a 500-pound bomb. Bicycles trapped too.

On again to a chateau on the outskirts where our aid station has been set up. Wounded pouring in. Litter calls. We go up a street blocked by a blown-up tank. Mines everywhere, under little piles of rock, in the open. Some walking wounded. "Some casualties up ahead." Two wounded. We put one on a litter and half carry the other. It's a long haul.

"Two more litters." OK, same trip over again. A dead Heinie in a dark green uniform. It looks like a woman to us. Shot out of a tree. It's dark now. Where the hell were those mines? Careful! Two men carry and one walks ahead to find the path. "Jesus, was that a mine?" We'd sure as hell know if it was.

Engineers, bulldozers working on the streets. It didn't look as though those streets could ever be used again, but those bulldozers are halfway through already. If they can't push it aside, they go over the top. Ammunition bearers going up all night long. Bullets for M-1s, bullets for machine guns, like water through a sieve. Bullets, bullets, bullets. We relay the wounded back from the aid station. The ambulances can't get through yet. Back past those dead Heinies, to the left and the first relief. Dear God, this is only one day of battle!

"Captain Matt wants you."

"Cross, I want you to go out to K Company as aid man. Better stock up your aid kits." Sgt. Tomasowitz says, "Don't take any unnecessary chances, take care of yourself. Have you got morphine? Know how to use it? Company K is over there—they're in reserve—report to Sgt. Brown."

I find the Sgt. And he introduces me to Lt. _____. "We jump off as spearhead at one o'clock." The boys are stretched out along a hedgerow. Some are writing and others are just sitting. The sergeants pass out bandoliers of ammo, hand grenades, and three rations. Writing might not be a bad idea. What can you say? What is written seems empty, feeble, but I put it in my helmet band.

Five minutes to go. Ready? Let's go. "Follow the Lt." they told me, so I stay close to the Lt.'s heels. We're over the first hedge and nothing has happened. We move up in a scattered line. Still nothing. Suddenly there are shots on the left and then on the right. That's where "I" and "L" companies are.[28] On ahead, breathless, tense, alert. Just like a

---

[28] By best estimates this action possibly takes place on July 27th and is the closest Cross and Fowler's accounts come to intersecting. Fowler would have been with L Company, which was on the left flank of Cross's position. L company was full of green soldiers—replacements for the heavy casualties of the previous days—who had frozen behind a hedgerow. Fowler was hit by a ricocheted bullet as he stood up out of cover to try to lead his men forward.

hunt, except this time the "game" shoots back. Down a little hill, surround a house, nothing here. A river, more like a wide creek, ahead. A bridge downstream about 100 yards, but the Lt. jumps in and wades. They told me to follow, so in to the waist and across. Out running through a meadow and halfway across there is a whistle crack of an 88. Thank Heaven I didn't try to make that bridge. Somebody is hit— the last man across. We get him into the shelter of the hill and find it's only a flesh wound in the calf of his leg. But I would have been behind him.

We move on slowly. It's getting dark, so we dig in around the edges of a small field. The Lt. comes by to check on casualties and we walk back towards the meadow but decide there aren't any more wounded. Back digging again. I am down about six inches when suddenly the sky lights up. Don't move! I remember if you stand still they may not see you. Here they come. Where was that big Kraut foxhole? Over there. When the flare fades, I run for it. Already seven or eight are in it, but there has to be room for one more. Bombs coming closer—all around us—must have got a lot of our boys. Anybody hurt? No answer, so I take a quick look around and decide we were lucky.

Back to the cellar, but no room to lie down. Sit all night with knees under my chin, cramps in my legs, and chilling cold. Next morning find bomb craters in a triangle pattern, not 100 feet from our foxhole.

Resume attack at 8:00 AM. Tiny hedgerow fields. Never see more than your head. We line up along a sunken road and go over the hedge in four or five different places. We're halfway through a wheat field when they open up. Burp guns and machine guns everywhere. "Medic! Medic!" It's the Lt. Hit in the arm, but not bad, and he'll keep going. Another lad close by is nicked, then a man back near the hedge. Base of the throat—a large Carlyle—really hit bad. Have to get him out of here—arm over my shoulder, half turn, crack, crack—brains all over me—great hole in his head. I get over the fence, but I don't know how. We move along the hedgerow—more men hit. Bandage, bandage, bandage. Both aid kits low. Got to get more supplies. Work with other companies along the sunken road. Bandage, morphine, gaping flesh wounds, sucking sounds. The bad ones don't complain, but one kid nicked makes an awful fuss. Must check and see how many litter cases. Go ahead one row and check right, then left. Kid dug in right in the corner of the hedgerow. Move away a few feet and crash—right in the corner. Run back, but there is nothing I can do. On to right again, over a hedge and—a dead man in every foxhole—shells must have come from behind. On along the hedge and—there are men standing looking at me—they are not GIs!! They are Germans! We must be to the right—run, run, run, over a hedge, across a field, another hedge, the sunken road—men in holes here too. All are dead—crossfire. Some SPs got behind us, we heard later.

This was bloody Sunday, July 29. Probably the worst day the 134th ever had. One shell in that road got the Major and four others. Took off the back of his head, but he still lived a little while. Blasovitch (came in with me) got it—he was loading an ambulance at the end of that sunken road. The Germans knew exactly where we were on their maps and caught us in a murderous crossfire.

We are in reserve. The Heinies seem to be falling back, fighting a rear-guard action. We move up slowly, checking every point—orchard, farm, woods. Dig in whenever we stop—four or five times a day, always some shelling around dusk. Nothing so chilling as an 88. Whistle, crack, and a crunching, rending sound. Feel like an insect and a blind giant swinging a club at you. Am I scared? You're damned right—there are no atheists here.

Must cross the Voire river. We swing right and go through a narrow pass with hills going up at forty-five degrees on both sides. One machine gun could wipe us out, but we see only a couple of scared Germans—kids, probably running away. Find a narrow spot where we cross on a ladder covered by a couple planks. Keep left of the road—mines on the right. We're across and start up a steep rocky path, scouts moving ahead. Crack! An 88. We scatter and dig. L Company tries on our right. They've hit something—machine guns, rifles, burp guns, 50 MMs. Quiet again. We're pulling back. There go two medics after L Company casualties. Should I go too? My company is moving. Maybe I'd better stay. Later I heard both those medics were killed.

Back to the road—we go straight up through the woods, dig in, then on again straight over. I follow Joe Kimberly, best soldier I ever saw. Through one field, halfway up another when all Hell breaks loose—that house is a damned pillbox! "Medic! Medic!"—one hit in the arm, another in the leg. Bandage and help to the hedge. Must be more hit. Try putting my jacket on a stick so the Red Cross can be seen. Start up left side of the field—crump, crump, crump—mortars—walk down the middle of the field.

Man hit in foot—can't walk—help him back to trail. Where the Hell is it? Must be this way. There are some buildings and then a German officer. Run, run. How could we get lost! "Hey, where is that aid station? What outfit is this?" "The 320th."

"Where is the 134th?" Must be left. Got to get back. Go along river a long way and finally meet litter bearers. K Company is left and higher up. Black as ink. Up, up, stumble and fall. Some buildings. K Company is straight ahead 200 yards. Finally find them and go to work on wounded. Two bad and five lightly hit. One boy has broken leg and broken arm, got to keep him warm. No blankets, but gather up discarded clothing. Nothing to do but wait for litter bearers. Crash, crash, crump. Whose are those—ours or theirs? Good God, it's both— theirs just barely over and ours just clearing us—never heard anything like this. How can they miss? 2:00 AM, the litter bearers—one team and two litters—aid man Taylor and I carry one. Cross a field, over some barbed wire, now down a trail. Feel with your feet. Stagger and slide. Half a mile more and we're on the road—the aid station? "Maybe a mile." It was two or three. Silent shapes along the road. Were they GIs? The aid station—it's 3:30 AM. Tired, numb, K Company wasn't wiped out, but they lost eighteen men.

Open country again. Jerry is falling back. We're moving somewhere on trucks. The 35th getting a rest? Rest, Hell, it's a long move. We're on the wrong road. Planes overhead, strafing and bombing, bombing the road we should have been on.

"Cross, I'm taking your place. You go in to the aid station." Nice clean-cut kid named Snowbreak from Minnesota. Killed in the attack his first day. He took my place!

Morphine, bandages, sulfa, splints—faster—there are so many— hurry—move them back—time may save their lives. This is not X-ray, but it's a reprieve after being an aid man. We didn't know at the time, but Mortaine was a huge trap—the Falaise pocket—and we were the stopper. An important victory and the end of one phase. It's Sunday and we're resting. I remember singing "Abide With Me" for the chaplain's service. A lot of men never paid much attention to church before.

The Germans are falling back, and we are moving rapidly by jeep. It's just like the movies—crowds line the small-town streets, waving flags and throwing flowers, apples, plums. Leo rolls cheese cans down the road, and we laugh as the kids scramble for them. People try to shake hands, throw kisses. It's exhilarating, but I keep thinking there must be a camera somewhere. Le Mans tops everything. This is a big town and it's delirious. Street cafes, curbs, swarming pretty girls. The Makee are a big help now. They know the country and where the Heinies are. The Germans are disorganized here. We capture replacements, who do not know where the front is. Stop at "Aix-en-Othe" while the woods are cleared ahead—thousands of prisoners—rest. The mayor of Le Mans gave us fresh eggs and a black-and-white puppy for a mascot.

Another sudden move. Stop on battlefield of First World War—old trenches, rusted bayonets, parts of rifles, gas masks. Advance on foot under scattered shelling. I receive a letter from my wife, Florence. Tells me we have a beautiful daughter, Carol, now a month old. Her picture looks like one of my baby pictures.

Set up aid station in a beer parlor. Bed down. Get orders to move at 10:30 PM. It's black as Hell. How can the drivers see? Seems we are following the Second Battalion. They've crossed the Mosel on a bridge and have been trapped, bridge blown behind them.

Out of the darkness—a jeep with a wounded man. Get him on a litter and work under blankets for blackout. He's hit hard, broken leg. Must get him to the hospital. Captain Matt points where the hospital should be and we move over crooked country roads, back through two villages. "Here's where we were." Turn right along the railroad. Can this be right? Up a hill through a village. Should be here, but it isn't. Back to the aid station. Try to make patient more comfortable, check maps and try again, this time after three hours we make it. Thank goodness, somebody has a bottle.

Daylight we catch up. Jeeps are off road just above Mosel. Shelling. Got to find cover. Left a half mile are deep woods. Dig in. One boy cut off with Second Battalion comes in. He hid all day in the brush watching German tanks and gun emplacements. At dark we swim river. Take him to Lt. Colonel. He was cited later for this.

Outposts in buildings along road leading to bridge. Under terrific shell fire. Litter call. Nothing to do but make a run for it in the jeep. Trees cut bare by shrapnel, branches on the road, but we get through. One man in ditch, two in a basement. Heavy shelling. Get one out, then the other. Shells bracket road behind us, but we're lucky.

Swing up river toward Nancy, which we take without too much trouble. Heinie artillery catches us on a narrow street, but our luck holds. Set up aid station in former schoolhouse. French band comes down the street. Snipers still shooting. Old gent on a bicycle—crump, crump—the old man is down. The band hits the dirt but nobody is hurt. All come back gesticulating wildly and covered with dirt.

Our infantry is attacking across the river and up the hill. Throw in white phosphorus. 50 MM machine guns chattering. Darkness. Big fuss about a casualty down on the river. Struggle through rubble and wade in for him. Turns out to be a Jerry with a light wound. Terrific haul to the top of mountain. Move slowly, carefully. May be under observation. Pick up three litter cases. One medic lay all night in a ditch, but not a whisper, "knew we'd come." Improvise litter from cellar door. Slip, slide, stumble, and we're down again.

Sugarloaf—a death trap. Open round, snow-covered knob. Try frontal attack. Mowed down. Finally circle and secure top, but at a terrible cost.

Spot a wounded Heinie lying in a field. Major Wood goes with us to get him. It's a GI, hit bad, but he's crawled over a mile. Out there all night and all day, but still strong. These kids have guts. Wants a cigarette and water.

Move forward slowly. Use backroads. Main roads are mined or blocked. Dig in, wait, then move into a small town knocked to Hell by planes. Heavy fighting on our right. Towns burning. Field littered with German dead. Allencourt, Gramercy Woods.

We are in a holding position. Aid station is in a big stone wine cellar. Hear a voice—"Well, the old bastard looks about the same." It's my brother, Glenn, hale and hearty. I haven't heard from him since before

D-Day. Didn't know whether he was alive or dead. His outfit is in Nancy, and I go back to spend the night with them. Weeks before, one of his buddies had found my pack in a field but never told Glenn. Now they had seen our "wagon wheel" patch and knew our regiment was in the area.[29] Glenn borrowed a jeep to run us down. Stopped to ask a sentry what was ahead. "Germans." He turned around and finally found us.

Our stone cellar was quite safe, but one morning a goose took a direct hit. Later the OP was shelled and a guard was hit in the throat. He came running, the blood spurting. Captain Matt managed to clamp the artery, but the boy died on the way to the Clearing Company.

One morning, snipers and burp guns sounded only yards away. Piper Cubs spotted the enemy forming in a field in the woods and called the location to our mortars, who miraculously had that spot zeroed in. These mortars saved us from capture. Here a shell dropped in front of La Salle, a California boy who had volunteered to be an aid man.

Again we moved up slowly through mud and water. Six consecutive aid stations were hit by shellfire, but luckily no one was injured. Captain Matt was spanked in the backside by a piece of shrapnel which came through a wooden wall and his sleeping bag. Mortars hit the room adjoining them as we worked over casualties and blew off the roof onto our trailers. On the move again, we were narrowly missed by 88s several times. Nothing can paralyze your mind like the scream, crunch of an 88.

Bloody Monday—Hill 108—We handled 138 casualties that day. The men were caught crossing a bald hill and mowed down. I had a boy emptying the water bucket where I washed my bloody hands as I worked over casualties.

Flint and I set up a forward aid station. A casualty reported up ahead, but directions were vague. Jeep returns after two hours. Got as far as a blown-out bridge. Tried again in an hour and brought back a lad with a broken leg, wounds right side, liver region, and upper lung. Freezing

---

[29] This was the shoulder badge of the 35th Division, under which the 134th Regiment served.

cold with faint pulse. We did all we could until the ambulance came, but I knew this one would never make it.

St. Jean—the convoy was caught by 88s and our trailer hit twice. I scrambled among some blocks of stone. Forest was hit. Shrapnel through a door in a basement cut the clothing from his arm and shoulder. Luckily, only a flesh wound. Forest came back later. That night it seemed impossible that the convoy wasn't smashed.

The litter bearers followed tanks in attack and Dugan was hit. Wasn't too bad, but Dugan never came back. The tankers had a rough day, caught in the open by artillery.

Puttelange—Second Battalion jumped off in the dark, waded a swollen river, and captured the Heinies in their foxholes, advanced through rough country over roads where even the jeeps stalled. Approached the Saar and the Heinies fell back desperately. The Saar was a natural barrier, which they knew how to defend. Our river bank was wide open and all bridges blown, but the infantry found what was left of a railroad bridge and made it across under a terrific pounding. The fighting moved on, but a stray mortar killed Tommy Tomasowitz. Tommy, who told me not to take any unnecessary chances. Tommy, who never shirked anything; he was a section sergeant and could have stayed further back.

Combat engineers, trying to put in a bridge under direct fire. Thill and I answer the call. A run by jeep for a mile or so on an open road above the river. A major waved us under a railway viaduct during a burst of shelling; as it slackened, we ripped across a canal and doubled back 100 yards to the bridgehead where the engineers were huddled behind a pitiful little jumble of masonry and girders. Two more barrages screamed in. We piled on five wounded men and Thill took off as fast as our cargo and the bombed roads would permit. Just got away when the shelling began again. Fifteen men, including the major, who directed us in, were hauled away from that bridge. My hat is off to the combat engineers.

Across the Saar we found our ex-mess sergeant drunk one night. He fired at a German plane with an M1, could have brought on a bombing raid, so he was sent to a line company. Got tanked up whenever possible. One day he started after a tank with a grease gun chattering when a mortar got him.

The move from the Saar to the Blies was one of the weirdest we ever made. Black as ink, over barely passable muddy roads with gun flashes splitting the darkness. Up around a burning house, a devil's torch which must have been visible for miles. Set up aid station in a surprisingly good house, well-built, interesting décor. "Tiny" stayed behind to guard the supplies we couldn't take. Tiny, always careful, never took any chances if he could help it. Stopped a couple days at regimental before he caught up with us. I was sitting by the telephone talking to the chaplain when there was a terrific explosion across the street. Six feet from us in a hall, a plate-sized piece of shrapnel sliced through Tiny's head. Big, fun-loving, careful Tiny. Nothing in ten months shook me like this. It was also too much for Captain Matt. Tiny had been his man Friday.

Assault boats arrive too late for the Third to cross the Blies, but the First got over and the Third followed. Bitter fighting here, for the Heinies were on higher ground. Newspaper correspondents got a taste of evacuation when Thill took one down the river there. Our boys worked under a Red Cross flag with some German medics. Several times they helped us and then returned to their lines. About 9:00 PM the aid station got a call. Troops pulling out of the village have a wounded man. Cherry and I start out in the jeep. It's pitch black and we are in the ditch in 50 yards. Ambulance pulls us out. We crawl along a muddy track to main road to turn off, and for two miles I walk in front of the jeep to find the road—pouring rain, deep mud, sporadic shelling. Finally, we find five men with bad feet and one with a strained back. They're having a feast of fried ham and potatoes. The rest of the troops are gone, and they are positive they took the "wounded" man. Two miles of mud and water to the main road and another mile to that burning house where the tankers are. It's 2:00 AM. Their surgeon gives us a "snifter." Back at the aid station, another hour, and there is a call threatening Captain Matt with court martial if that man isn't picked up. We're too beat to go back, so another crew starts off. They got their man. He'd shot himself in the foot. The officer who threatened Captain Matt did the same thing later on.

The Blies, our aid station is in a basement room at the end of a bridge the Heinies are trying to knock out. Several civilian refugees, including a German girl, play guitar and sing "Pennies from Heaven." We are in French territory, but across the river is Germany. Finally, the Heinies are pushed back up the hill, and we move over into Germany to an advance aid station Ozzie and the boys have set up. Ozzie is sick and Flint takes over. Buildings are flimsy, but the shelling is mostly directed at the bridge. I come down with something, which the surgeon says is pneumonia, but I persuade them not to send me in, as I might not get back to the outfit again. Sulfa and a few days in bed seem to knock it out.

Another outfit is taking over and we pull back across the Biles. Day and night chatter of a machine gun covering a pillbox. Intermittent shelling. One man killed around the corner and another hit bad. New replacements get baptism—one is a Master Sgt. who has goofed somewhere and this is his punishment. He's really scared.

Fighting here is fierce and promises to get worse, with Germans holding on to Saarbrucken desperately. Word of their breakthrough in the north doesn't sound good.

A long move—the whole division. Bitterly cold, mountains dark and forbidding. Keep interval, watch for planes. The 137th was strafed on this move. Sign reads so many miles to Metz—this has to be the "Bulge." We stop in Metz for Christmas in barracks and have a wonderful turkey dinner. Bill Brown, Lundmark, Waldower, and I harmonize on White Christmas and Sgt. Marko stuffs us with turkey. Metz is a part of the Maginot Line. Forts all around—guns pointing the wrong way.

Move on north—Luxemburg and Belgium. Bastogne is somewhere ahead. "The armor has broken through." Ambulance after ambulance speeds by.

It's a winter wonderland. We set up in the summer palace of King Albert of Belgium. Beautiful stone chateau—thank God for the stone, as building's hit several times—but we're inside. The infantry is out in the snowdrifts. It is bitter cold.

Sainlez knocked to Hell. Old man with hands tied, shot to death. Many civilians died in fire. Half a mile from chateau, German mortars hit a barn full of GIs. Twenty hurt bad—two killed.

Every man except medics is armed. Jerry is closing in. We make plans to run for it. Tank and half-track guns chatter all around us. One German tank is hit and medics bring in five wounded. Sentry detects movement in woods, calls for artillery, and we find thirteen dead, including three artillery observers. Minutes more and they would have been calling big stuff in on us.

Through the woods about a mile and a half is "Lutrebois." We trade it back and forth several times. Artillery catches eleven Heinie tanks lined up in a row. Planes get eight more. Bless those Piper Cub observers.

Wounded civilians in Lutrebois. We've got to get them out. We go in at night. At the edge of the woods we sweat out a barrage, then start across an open field. Woo-woo-woo screaming mimmies. Express train through the air, blood curdling. Keep away from the path—it's mined. The people are in one big basement—one Heinie and seven civilians. I help an old lady, about seventy-five, her pitiful belongings wrapped in a tablecloth. She slips and slides, goes to her knees a dozen times as I half carry her up that twisting, icy trail. It's bitter cold but I am dripping wet. More shells, more mimmies, and then here is the jeep. We have made it.

One of the survivors is a girl. She hesitates, then strips off her dress. She is hit in the side. Her father's arm is green and stinks. Sulfa, bandage, and on to collecting.

Lutrebois is finally ours. Dead men piled like cordwood. These Heinies are SS men. Some of our boys found with 38s shoved down their throats. One of our aid men, Lerner from Brooklyn, didn't make it back.

The 137th relieves us and we rest for two days, then swing in a pincer on woods beyond Lutrebois. Beautiful barrage, as infantry and tanks advance, forcing SS to fall back. We push to highway and are pinched out. Bitter weather. One boy crawled into the station, his feet blocks of ice. While I work on his feet, he tells me his buddy standing behind me is nuts. He is holding a rifle butt in his hands. We talk him into taking some "blue bombers," and he is out like a light. Whew!

Walking outside the aid station, I hear a shot close by. A GI has shot himself in the foot. One replacement claims he can't see. The first Sgt., determined the man was faking, handed him a rifle, saying: "There is no one between you and the Germans—you'd better see."

Blasted, burned out US armor everywhere. Stacks of dead waiting to be hauled away. This is by far the worst US disaster we have seen. The enemy was trying to get gasoline and was stopped only some hundreds of yards from one of the biggest fuel dumps in Europe. Hitler's last big gamble didn't quite make it.

From the Bulge we moved down near Linne, Belgium, for a brief rest period. On up over a great snowy waste into Hooperdang on the Our river where we sit and look at the Heinies on the other side. This was a holding position, but our outposts catch murderous fire occasionally. A bomb leveled half the building the aid station is in. Two dead oxen and a police dog ripening in spite of the cold.

The first of February we were relieved and swung north through Belgium into Germany through a British section where we saw the devastating results of the British attack. In what had been a handsome border town not an undamaged building remained. Fields dotted with shell holes and dead cattle. Mines everywhere, with only a narrow track cleared. On ever-greasy, horrible roads in streaking rain to Randerath on the banks of the Rohr, which was at flood state because of a blasted dam upstream. Here we sat for almost three weeks under heavy shell fire, waiting for the floods to abate. Apparently, the Germans were using huge slag piles for observation. Our aid station was in a thin shell of a building, and we usually had chow outside. One morning, after heavier shelling than usual, Sgt. Ozzie had it put inside. Fergy decided to go outside to eat when a terrific explosion rocked the whole building. A big 240 MM landed in the street forty feet from the door. Fergy was twenty feet from the blast, but miraculously the shrapnel went up and over his head. He wasn't scratched, although one eardrum was damaged. Across the street First Sgt. Hill, looking out the window, caught the blast in the face. He lost an eye.

Here we heard our first V bombs. The motors sounded like huge souped-up motorcycles. You held your breath, hoping they'd keep going over. One night, one cut out suddenly, silence, and then a jarring blast. Two miles away this one wiped out a gun emplacement, killing five men and leaving a hole big enough for a house. This area was dotted with German pillboxes. One day I counted fifteen without moving an inch.

Finally, the flooded Rohr went down and we "jumped" across. That day Conger crawled out to a wounded buddy lying in a ditch. He couldn't apply the bandage in the ditch, so in spite of the pleadings of the man, he sat up on the edge and worked. A sniper's bullet caught him in the side. He was brought in, apologizing for not doing a better job. Conger came through OK, but the doctors told him an inch one way would have hit his spine and an inch the other way would have hit his liver. Either would have been curtains.

The Heinie troops here were a ragtag lot and surrendered in droves, but they had sowed mines like wheat. One hour, I took care of two men with feet missing. Here we worked with some colored tankers who were terrific. It was their first time in combat, and they just "barrel-assed." Those boys did a wonderful job.

One night move I will never forget. No moves were good, but night moves were always bad. You crept along, stopped, crept some more, stopped, sure all the time any minute the Heinies would find the convoy strung out like sitting ducks. This night we moved like a snail with terrific cannonades lighting the horizon in sudden flashes. Screaming mimmies moaned and we hit the ditch—only there wasn't any ditch. No cover at all. Shells screamed overhead and plowed the field just short of us. A route guide helped us by saying, "They're shelling the next turn." At that turn the convoy stalled. Just ahead a shell crashed and an anti-tank gunner was killed. Slowly we crawled, finally reaching a shack glorified into an aid station. At least we were inside, but there were twenty-nine men in two small rooms and a tiny basement.

I finally slept on a pile of potatoes, certainly the worst bed I ever had. The shelling was almost continuous. Usually one could identify our own guns, but that night they all sounded like German guns.

The infantry pushed off at dawn, sending back long lines of dejected "supermen." At an advance station the boys heard a murderous creeping barrage coming in on the flank. It ripped, tore and plowed the earth until not a living thing survived. From that direction it couldn't be ours—was it German? The boys watched, fascinated, and almost danced when they saw Canadian infantry advancing through the smoke. That afternoon I rode over some of that area and have never seen such unbelievable destruction. Orchards were jagged snags and fields were churned, raw earth. This was the Wesel pocket where, together with the Canadians, we finally pushed the Heinies across the Rhine.

Now came a real honest-to-God ten-day rest period at Brook, back near the edge of Holland, where we played softball, went to Leige, and saw our crazy jeep driver, Thill, get his *coup de grace*. We had radios or speakers in every room. I helped organize a battalion show and soaked up the sunshine.

March 25th, we started moving east again. The Rhine was ahead and we knew it had been crossed somewhere. Ammunition lined the road for miles. In the early afternoon it got smoky, and we suddenly thought of smoke screens. It was murky dusk when we stopped, apparently just short of the Rhine, and heard there were pontoon bridges ahead. Tracers fingered the sky and red balls of anti-aircraft floated lazily overhead.

When do we cross? Tonight! This is it. The last big barrier where the Germans must fight or lose. From Normandy on, this has been our goal and here it is. We moved up slowly in trucks, jeeps, gun carriers, and on foot over a slight rise, and ahead was the baleful glare of a huge searchlight poking straight away. What the Hell is that? A perfect target! But the light was up the river and against it we could suddenly see our way—that narrow black thread, a murky torrent, tiny silhouetted figures directing the troops waiting to cross.

We're on the pontoon bridge. Overhead a plane roars and strafes. Red dotted lines rise and fall in the blackness. Red balloons float up and away. Ahead riflemen are shooting into the water. Is it boats, mines, Jerry frogmen? The riflemen kneel and shoot at anything that moves.

We're across and up the other side. There is a roar and the hideous chatter of strafing machine guns. The roaring death is diving, it's over and away. We've scattered like quail and nobody is hit. Ahead, a whole town is burning, and we creep through like ghouls. Shells smashing ahead. We swing left to black buildings where we set up the station and gratefully spread our blankets.

At daylight we move on again. A wrecked American tank with the tanker's body smoldering beside the turret. He helped knock out a whole Heinie artillery battery before they got him. Two hundred yards away are a dozen 88s surrounded by dead Heinies.

A steady stream of wounded—scissors, sulfa, bandages, splints, and morphine. After dark we push through horrible bogging and under shrieking shellfire to an isolated farmhouse. In the morning there are two little German girls, horribly wounded. One has a piece of black shrapnel where her eye should be—dried bloody bandages sticking from torn flesh. There would be no war if people could see this or those boys who came in one morning with no faces. From forehead to chin there was nothing. One could still talk, and you could see his throat and larynx move. The flesh that had been a face hung in a bloody swinging flap.

The 35th is pressing in on the northern edge of the Ruhr valley, which is a scattered forest of smokestacks as far as the eye can reach, and we see more evidence of the terrible efficiency of our bombs. There is an awful sameness to Germany's industrial cities. The heart of each is a smashed, burned-out desolation of twisted steel and ruptured masonry.

At Gladbeck, thousands of civilians are huddled in a coal mine. Women, children, and old men seeking shelter in the dripping, smelly black tunnels. Kirchen has been hit hard. Dazed civilians can't understand what has happened. To escape shellfire, we burst into a house where the owners try to argue. What kind of dopes do they take us for? That Mosel wine they didn't offer us was delicious. The Nazi headquarters next door provided a field day for souvenir hunters—guns, knives, swords. Ray got a beautiful shotgun, and Chappie, a brand new .45. A Nazi souvenir shop had every Heinie emblem you ever saw. They were not exactly salable items now.

Bochum is knocked to pieces. The center of the city a tumbled wasteland with a few cellars still habitable. We push the Germans across the river and pull back to Buer Resse, which is on the Herne Ems Canal. There is a slave-labor camp here. A mine, where we find some pitiful human wrecks wasted by disease and starvation. Vacant faces and dead eyes. The contractor who should have been feeding these prisoners had been selling the food on the black market.

Pop Mertons, who speaks fluent German, goes through a tunnel into the town and finds it is held by a small group of Heinies. The civilians want to surrender. A wrecked railroad span is bridged by one of the boys swimming across, towing a boat into the break. To the right the engineers have gotten a Bailey bridge across under a smoke screen.

Finally, we are squeezed out as the Rhur pocket shrinks, and we take off on a long, motorized move eastward. We are traveling through territory already taken, and the most striking sight is DPs thronging the roads. Literally thousands of people are on the move on foot, carrying their meager possessions on their backs or pulling small wagons. Larger wagons stacked with pooled possessions are pushed or pulled by eight to ten people. Sometimes an antique tractor tows three or four wagons, and there is a sprinkling of ancient cars crawling along with blow-out and engine trouble at every turn. French, Dutch, Poles, Russians—ragged suffering humanity, but smiling and happy to be free and going home.

An advance party tears into a town and is stopped by German sentries. Our boys do some fast talking. The German soldiers want to quit, but their officer wants to fight. He finally agrees to surrender to a ranking officer.

We stay overnight in a small village, and as we are loading up next morning there is a roar of planes—Heinie planes. Our ack-ack begins to chatter as two go over, and a third blooms smoke, and a parachute billows as the plane noses straight toward us. We scramble for shelter as the plane crashes a hundred yards away. No bombs aboard, thank God, but machine guns still crackle for a while.

The Elbe river—60 miles to Berlin. We hear the Second Armored got across and were chopped up. Crossing here could be rough. Finally, we get the word. This is a holding position. We are to wait for the Russians! Dear God, we have made it. The worst has got to be over. A few shells, a couple of raids, but this is a holding position—we wait here.

K Company is attacked by a raiding party. Two men in the outpost are killed. A bazooka goes straight through a room full of men, but no one is hit. The men swear a woman was calling the orders for the Heinies.

The Germans attack at another point. They crossed and came in behind our position, but the boys were on their toes and of the raiding party twenty were killed, twenty wounded, and twenty captured. Among the seriously wounded was a fifteen-year-old boy who was second in command. He said he had been in our village watching the boys play football. If anyone looked suspicious, he would ask for a cigarette.

We wait for the Russians to reach Berlin, and now the only thing that matters is "points." Thank God for five battle stars, my wife and daughter at home, and my age. The war is over for me, and soon I will be going home.

Conclusion
By William G. Cross

Dad was one of the lucky ones who made it back safely from the war. A singer in New York doing spots on live radio prior to entering the service, he returned to continue his singing career while moving and settling in East Haddam, Connecticut. A decade and a half later, still involved in music, he, along with his brother Glenn Cross, who is also mentioned in the diary, became two of the twenty-five men who made up the chorus for the popular early 60s television show Sing Along With Mitch.

Dad enjoyed his work very much and in his later years seemed to be content to live a peaceful, quiet life in the beautiful countryside surrounding his East Haddam home. He passed away in 1973.

He is survived by his daughter, Carol Cross, and son, Bill Cross of East Haddam, Connecticut, as well as two granddaughters, Kelly Cross and Katelyn Cross.

PART III

The Photography of Gordon Edward Cross

What follows are the photographs of Gordon Edward Cross, taken throughout the time of his deployment in Europe. As a professional photographer, Gordon had his camera on him frequently, but time (and safety) to take pictures was in short supply. With no darkroom available, he could not develop the pictures until he returned to the States, so the information we have on each photo is scant—the words accompanying each picture read more like titles than captions. But we have done our best to preserve Gordon's voice by leaving them mostly unchanged.

The brevity of words itself captures the speed with which the 134th was racing across Europe, from France, to Belgium, and into Germany; from one battlefield to the next, into one shattered city then another. Gordon's words for the sights and places turned out to be as stark as the bombed-out ruins themselves. The desolation, even rendered in black and white, is visceral. The photos of German dead, a torched tank, of shattered homes, churches, factories, form a grim landscape of human-made violence and human-made loss.

Ever the artist, Gordon preserved for us more than a series of unrelated or unconnected images. Studying them, a story emerges—of young men, foreigners in a strange land, of soldiers doing their duty and encountering Poles, French, Dutch, Belgians, Russians, Germans alike—even forming unexpected friendships in the process. For these young men from small Midwest towns, the cobblestone streets, bucolic villages, medieval cathedrals, expansive chateaus—bombed out or not—would have felt foreign indeed.

But there would have been an undeniable familiarity in these settings, too. One can sense a familiar small-town solidarity and rural pace in the villages and countryside that Gordon captures. The feel of these places must have resonated with these Midwestern men in the brief respites between the hellfire of battle. The GIs must have perceived it when they met the liberated residents, who offered cheers, toasts, pies, smiles (and sometimes more).

I can only imagine that these moments of recognition reminded these men of the 35th Division, and the 134th Regiment within it, of why they were fighting in the first place. As the guns began to go silent, the rain of bombs stopped falling, and the enemy surrendered—cooperating more often than giving resistance—one sees in Gordon's photos everyday life reasserting itself. It comes in strange juxtapositions: American GIs walking amid foot traffic in a narrow medieval street, a farmer leading his oxen past an abandoned anti-aircraft gun, a woman riding a bike through a town square, GIs with rifles replaced by civilians with shopping bags. Gordon captures the humanity of people in the midst of, and emerging from, conflict. All these years later, we can bear witness to it, whether in the wary gaze of the photographer as he encounters German prisoners, a female Red Cross worker providing a haircut, a soldier cradling a puppy-turned-mascot, or an American medic holding a Belgian girl whose skinned knee he has just bandaged.

Finally, the pictures of the medics' and soldiers' homecoming show a triumphant but bittersweet return. The absence of so many friends and comrades, who had departed alongside but were not there upon return, would have been a heavy burden, even in the midst of great joy. Of these photos, one of the last is most striking to me. It is one Gordon took of the men on deck. The finer details of the shore are lost to focus, the ship still too far out in the harbor to pick out any family members waiting quayside. Before the jolt of return and reunion, you can almost feel their pensiveness. One man lights a cigarette, perhaps to counter his impatience, to calm his nerves, or both. The other men lean over the railing, peering into their home and—I'd like to think— the life ahead of them, as if trying to bring into focus their futures, the way one might look to a crowd of faces on the shore to pick out someone familiar—a brother, a sister, a wife, a child, the people, the places, resolving into the future to which they would belong.

For Gordon and his brother Glenn, who had also served in the 35th Division, the years ahead were full ones, with family, work—and success in both. Pictures of Gordon and Glenn and their post-war careers are included here, too. The photo of Gordon with his camera on set with Mitch Miller is another favorite of mine. I feel that the expression on Gordon's face captures a hard-earned steadfastness and a well-won confidence. As Gordon holds his camera in the midst of this musical show, I'm reminded once again of that artist's soul that sits within him. It is a big heart that looks out from those eyes.

I've also included a last picture of Bill, Gordon's son. In the photo, Bill stands next to a WWII-era jeep he restored. He tells me it was a bit of a weekend hobby, but I see it as more. It's a fitting sign of his stewardship of his father's legacy and a tribute to the vehicle that carried Gordon across France. I felt it only proper to include it. The photo is a salient reminder, for me, of the role Bill played preserving his father's extraordinary story. The medic's diary is writing that sits on the heart like a bright and burning ember. Its imagery remains top of mind long after reading. The same can be said for the story told through Gordon's photographs and the further shape of his life afterwards. For Gordon and Bill, I'm grateful.

May we all be so lucky to rise to the occasion as the men of the 134th did, to go out and face down fear, to accomplish the tasks that honor and loyalty put before us, then to return home. May we be lucky enough to gaze out on our lives ahead, like they did on the deck of their homecoming ship, knowing our good deeds are behind us but many more before us. May we all be as good stewards as Bill, preserving the memory of these men and their generation, lest we forget.

~ Ted Neill ~

134ᵗʰ Medical Group

At Sea

Boys Playing Ball

Pop – Combat Soldier

Soldier

Big German Gun - 240mm

Downed German Plane

France

On Patrol

Infantry Riding Tanks

Ambulance in France

Eye Inspection

German Casualty

Sundown

Mascot

Farm at Gramercy Woods

Major Townley and Big Boss

The Bulge

Bulge

The Bulge

The Bulge

Bulge

Camp Top Hat: Antwerp

Antwerp Waterfront

Buzz Bomb Damage, Leige

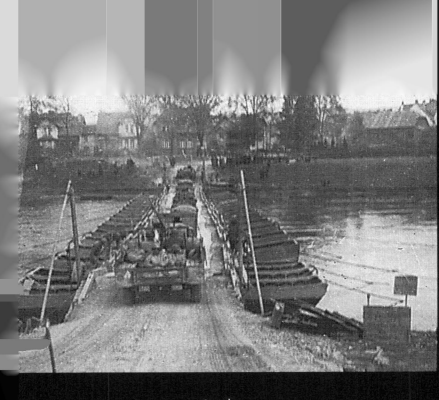

Aachen

St. Florentine

St. Florentine

Marburg

Marburg

Kessel

Hanover

Hanover

Gestapo HQ (Salvo, Boblick, Batson)

Bochum – Ruhr

Village where Nazi Party was organized

German village near Karlsruhe, Germany

Russian D.P.s

Fraternization

Woman Biking

Headed Home A.P. Hill

Welcome Home Serenade

Home

Welcome Home

Gordon Cross with Mitch Miller

Brothers Glen Cross and Gordon Cross with Mitch Miller on the set of the Mitch Miller show

Bill Cross
(Gordon's Son)

Appendix

Members of 134th Regiment Mentioned in Robert Fowler's Account

(in order of appearance)

Osborne, Albert: Sergeant, later Lieutenant—Worked as a window-dresser at Kresge's store in Omaha. He recruited and signed up Robert Fowler in 1937, when Fowler was sixteen.

Burmeister, ----: First Sergeant. Commented that Fowler did not "look eighteen" when he signed up (but let him sign up anyway).

Gidley, Kenneth: PFC and later Corporal—Fowler's first squad leader. It was Corporal Gidley whose stripes Fowler would receive at the time Gidley was inexplicably demoted from squad leader and Fowler became a squad leader corporal in his place. This was something Fowler always had mixed feelings about since it was at the misfortune of someone he liked and respected that he received this promotion.

Thompson, "Al" Albert: Captain—Company commander of 134th in 1937 when Fowler signed up. Eventually reassigned to Regimental Headquarters as adjunct.

Kelso, Earl H.: First Lieutenant, later Captain and company commander of L Company—platoon leader of the 134th in 1937 when Fowler signed up.

Gibson, "Gibby" Clinton: Sergeant—Mess sergeant and UP blacksmith.

Samson, Leo: Corporal and later Sergeant: Fowler's lifelong best friend.

Hall, Wallace B.: First Lieutenant and later Executive Officer.

Fowler, "Jim" James: Robert Fowler's younger brother who signed up in 1940, also at the age of sixteen.

Jelinek, Joe: Sergeant—Assigned as first sergeant along with Robert Fowler to act as instructors in March 1941, providing basic training to new recruits.

Boatsman, ----: First Lieutenant—Acting commander for Fowler in spring of 1941. Boatsman would go on to become Regional Commander in combat.

Mason, "Fran" Francis: Second Lieutenant—Acting commander for Fowler in spring of 1941. Mason would go on to be company commander and earned a reputation as an outstanding leader in combat.

Thurman, Ray: Captain—Transferred to command Rifle Company L in 1941 when Captain Kelso was transferred to Rifle Company A. Fowler remembered Captain Thurman as kind, friendly, and patient and someone who taught him a great deal.

Larson, Moose: First Lieutenant—Acting commander for L Company while training in Louisiana in August 1941. A man of large stature and, at times, formidable temper.

Lear, Ben: Lieutenant General—Lear was on the golf course in October 1941 when men of the 35th Division marched past and catcalled some women playing on the greens. The entire division faced disciplinary measures afterwards.

Ryan, Tom: Sergeant—Close friend of Robert and Jim Fowler.

Blunk, Jack: Accompanied Jim Fowler and Tom Ryan on pass the weekend of December 6-7th, 1941. The three men brought news back that all troops on furlough were to return to camp immediately.

Jacobs, Paul H.: Captain—Company commander, assigned December 1941 before shipping out to California. Also audited books for company fund.

Cantoni, John: Sergeant—When John Cantoni's boat capsized in the Cumberland River during winter maneuvers in Tennessee in 1944, he personally guided each man back to shore, returning to the deep and cold water repeatedly, even though he could not swim. Captain Lassiter recommended Sergeant Cantoni for the Soldier's Medal. Later, in combat outside St. Lo, Cantoni was shot through the lung but survived.

Lassiter, James: Captain—aka Jungle Jim. Recommended Sergeant Cantoni for the Soldier's Medal and was company leader throughout training and through combat in Europe. Reprimanded Fowler July 26th, 1944, when the Second Platoon, under the command of shavetail Lieutenant Stevens left the line of departure (LD) early.

Boggs, Dolan: Sergeant—Fowler trained Boggs as his understudy to be a platoon guide in 1943.

Thompson, Alfred: Captain and later Colonel—Thompson and Captain Lassiter were impressed with Fowler's map-reading abilities, and both officers were instrumental in promoting him to be a platoon guide in 1943.

McAllister, Robert: Captain—Appointed along with Fowler and Cantoni by Captain Lassiter to liquidate the "underground company fund" before embarkation to Europe. A dance "with pretty girls" followed.

Wright, Wes: Visited Jack Dempsey's restaurant, Greenwich Village, and got lost on the New York subway system with Fowler in April 1944, shortly before embarkation to Europe. Shot through the neck July 15th during attack on Hill 122.

Greenlief, Francis: Lieutenant, later General—Led First Platoon during the attack on Hill 122 and the taking of St. Lo.

Dailey, Lou: Second Lieutenant—Played in the backfield with Fowler during football games in Cornwall while awaiting deployment to Normandy. Was wiry, intelligent, and likable. He served for a time with the Second Battalion when they were stationed in the Aleutian Islands.

After training at OCS, he was promoted to second lieutenant and was well respected as a leader. KIA on July 16th.

McManaman, Ralph: Sergeant—Played in the backfield with Fowler during football games in Cornwall while awaiting deployment to Normandy. KIA July 17, 1944.

Bradley, Omar: Lieutenant General—Commander of the XIX Corp, First Army, which included the 134th Regiment after landing in Normandy.

Miltenberger, Butler: Colonel—Met with all senior sergeants the night of July 13, 1944, before the assault on Hill 122, passing on tips for combat and reiterating the importance of capturing the hill and St. Lo.

Owens, "Mole" Roscoe: Private First Class—Called up to neutralize an enemy machine gun nest on July 15th, when commanders of the Third Battalion realized their right flank was exposed. Received minor injuries while doing so along with Colonel Thompson.

Quinn, John: Private First Class—KIA by bullet to the head while attempting to neutralize enemy machine gun nest on July 15th, when commanders of the Third Battalion realized their right flank was exposed.

Wyant, ----: Major—Took command of the Third Battalion on July 15th when they became cut off from Colonel Thompson and his group of men.

Lloyd, Matt: Sergeant—Leader in the Third Platoon, in communication with Fowler during fighting on July 17th. Gave Fowler word to pull back after his platoon had inflicted heavy casualties on the enemy but had sustained many of their own. Accompanied Fowler on July 18th as part of a combat patrol to the rear to retrieve badly needed supplies.

Pennington, "Penny" Marion: Private First Class—Mobilized with Fowler on December 23, 1940. His civilian job had been as an elevator operator at the local YWCA building, and he joined the National Guard to "fight for his country." He was pink faced, pudgy, and uncoordinated when he enlisted. In the face of the German counterattack on July 17th, he demonstrated extraordinary courage. So much so that even when the men around him were unwilling to return fire, he was first up to do so. Fowler gave Penny his own M1 when Penny's ran out of ammo. He was among the six of the original forty-two members of the Third Platoon to survive the attack on Hill 122.

Campbell, John: Lieutenant—Friend of Fowler, member of Third Platoon with Leo Samson.

Sokol, Jerry: Sergeant—Took command of Weapons Platoon on July 17th when an artillery shell hit a tree above their platoon leader, and (although physically uninjured) he went berserk and started running around in circles, chasing imaginary enemy.

George Tiedje, John Quinn, Dick Campbell, Michael Pelegrino: Names mentioned among "several others" who were KIA during attack on Hill 122 and whose loss weighed so heavily on Fowler that he wept "like a baby."

Grobe, "Al" Albert: Private First Class—Accompanied Fowler on July 18th as part of a combat patrol to the rear to retrieve badly needed supplies.

Sass, Jake: Sergeant—July 18th, took a patrol down along the road toward St. Lo until he encountered the enemy. He returned and passed on the location where enemy fire had come from.

Weeks, Gordon: Sergeant—Accompanied Fowler with BAR (Browning automatic rifle) down sunken trail on attack July 18th. Fowler would later try to persuade his best friend, Leo Samson, platoon leader of the Third Platoon, to allow Weeks to be reassigned to the Second Platoon after the First and Second Platoons suffered over fifty percent casualties. Samson declined, as he thought Weeks was too needed in the Third.

Bailey, "Bill" William: Private First Class—Accompanied Fowler with BAR (Browning automatic rifle) down sunken trail on attack July 18th.

Tombrink, "Bill" William: Sergeant—KIA July 18th during German counterattack on Second Platoon as they held position on sunken trail.

Micelli, "Pat" Patrick: Sergeant—KIA July 18th during German counterattack on Second Platoon as they held position on sunken trail.

Gill, Chester: Sergeant—One of six of the original forty-two members of the Third Platoon that survived the taking of Hill 122. Fowler recommended Gill to replace him when he was shot.

Teply, Eddie: Sergeant—One of six of the original forty-two members of the Third Platoon that survived the taking of Hill 122.

Klentz, Robert: Sergeant—One of six of the original forty-two members of the Third Platoon that survived the taking of Hill 122.

Stevens, James: Lieutenant—New lieutenant assigned to Second Platoon Company L while on reserve July 20-21st, 1944.

Gallagher, ----: Lieutenant—New lieutenant assigned to First Platoon Company L while on reserve July 20-21st, 1944.

Brown, Buster: Sergeant—Originally thought KIA because of erroneous report. Fowler and other squad leaders initially wanted to recommend him for the Distinguished Service Cross for his bravery under fire.

★ Special Thanks ★

Much love and gratitude to the Fowler family, who assisted in the caretaking and preservation of this manuscript and also for providing photos and additional information. A special thanks to Roberta Russo and Colonel Robert Bloomquist for their continuing efforts to archive the history of the 134th through the 134th Infantry Regiment website http://www.coulthart.com/134/ and their commitment to maintaining the community of friends, family, and other loved ones with connections to the men of the 134th and their descendants.

Thanks to Steve Olson, Jack Hoban, and Edward Tick for their commitment to the wellbeing of the men and women who answer the call to be warriors and their striving for a higher ideal—an ideal we all can learn from. Thank you to everyone directly and indirectly involved in the efforts to keep the memory of these men, their courage, and their sacrifices alive and not lost to history.

A special thanks to the surviving children of Bob and Evelyn Fowler, my mother Kathleen, my aunts Mary Anne, Elyse, Margie, and Sally, as well as my cousins. This is your story as much as it is mine, and I'm grateful for your trust in telling it.

A deep, profound thanks to Bill Cross and the family for their generosity in sharing Gordon's story, archiving his photographs, and their continuing efforts to ensure his story was not lost to history.

And finally, a sincere word of gratitude and an acknowledgement to Robert Lewis Fowler and Gordon Edward Cross, who sacrificed so others would not have to. Your words echo through the years to still move us today. We are in your debt.

★ Please Consider Supporting ★

Veterans Crisis Line https://www.veteranscrisisline.net/

If you are a veteran in crisis or know one who is, you are not alone. You can visit the site above or call 1-800-273-8255.

The US Veterans Administration has found that in 2018 approximately 22 veterans take their lives *daily.*[30] That is a rate of one man or woman's death almost every hour. In the US, since the wars in Iraq and Afghanistan, *there are many years that we lose more soldiers and veterans to suicide than combat.*[31] This does not even include deaths from accidental drug overdoses or alcohol related deaths.

Th free support offered by Veterans Crisis Line is confidential and available every day 24/7. These services are available to all veterans all service members, all members of the National Guard and Reserve, as well as their family members and friends.

If you are not a service member and have never visited your local VA Hospital, or considered volunteering or helping in any way available to you, please do. Veterans, sacrificed, and carry the burdens of trauma and loss, so we don't have to. They have lived up to the highest ideals of our country but tragically receive little of the support and recognition they deserve once the guns go silent and the news cycle has moved on. We can honor their service with our own service, our own compassion, and the understanding and gratitude that we offer to them. *#BeThere* for a veteran.

---

[30] https://www.mentalhealth.va.gov/suicide_prevention/index.asp
[31] https://www.va.gov/opa/pressrel/pressrelease.cfm?id=2951

Soldier's Heart: Transforming the Heart and Soul Wounds of War https://www.soldiersheart.net/

Founded by Edward Tick, PhD, Soldier's Heart's mission is to transform the emotional, moral, and spiritual wounds that often result from war and military service. They help active-duty troops and veterans develop new and honorable warrior identities. They offer genuine homecoming, reintegration, and a path for post-traumatic growth. They also empower and equip families, care providers, individuals, and communities to support our troops and veterans as they work to establish new identities.

Soldier's Heart has developed a proven holistic, community-based, spiritual method of healing that goes beyond conventional treatment methods. Their methods incorporate what they have learned from intensive study of world-wide spiritual traditions, indigenous cultures, mythology, and warrior traditions. Countless veterans and members of the military have experienced significant and lasting healing after working with them. Thousands of chaplains and behavioral health professionals from the US Army, Air Force, National Guard, and Special Operations forces have received training from Soldier's Heart. They offer retreats that create a safe place for veterans and active-duty servicemen and women to share their military experiences. They also offer family retreats, workshops, trainings, educational programs, and lectures on a wide variety of topics.

Wounded Warrior Project
https://www.woundedwarriorproject.org/

Veterans and service members who incurred a physical or mental injury, illness, or wound while serving in the military on or after September 11, 2001, are the focus of the WWP. The wellbeing of these men and women is the mission.

The WWP provides services and support to veterans, service members, and their families, incorporating them into a community that understands them and provides help for free—because there is no dollar value to the service they have provided, no price to put on finding recovery, and no limit to what wounded warriors can achieve.
There have been more than 52,000 servicemen and women physically injured in recent military conflicts. About 500,000 live with invisible wounds, from depression to post-traumatic stress disorder. Upwards of 320,000 experience debilitating brain trauma. Advancements in technology and medicine save lives—but the quality of those lives might be profoundly altered.

The numbers speak for themselves, because not every warrior can. With the support of a community of donors and team members, the Wounded Warrior Project gives a voice to the needs of veterans and service members, empowering them to begin the journey to recovery.

Made in the USA
Columbia, SC
09 May 2019